Grace's Window

P9-CQW-679

GRACE'S WINDOW

♦ Entering the Seasons of Prayer ♦

Suzanne Guthrie

COWLEY PUBLICATIONS
Cambridge ♦ Boston
Massachusetts

© 1996 by Suzanne Guthrie.
All rights reserved.

Published in the United States of America by Cowley Publications, a division of the Society of St. John the Evangelist. No portion of this book may be reproduced, stored in or introduced into a retrieval system, or transmitted, in any form or by any means—including photocopying—without the prior written permission of Cowley Publications, except in the case of brief quotations embodied in critical articles and reviews.

Library of Congress Cataloging-in-Publication Data:
Guthrie, Suzanne, 1951–
    Grace's window: entering the seasons of prayer / Suzanne Guthrie.
       p.   cm.
    ISBN: 1-56101-124-X (alk. paper)
    1. Church year meditations. I. Title.
BV30.G847   1996
242'.3—dc20   95-44799
                                                                    CIP

Portions of "First Love," "Crosswalk," "Practice Time," "Noon Office," "The Music of Loneliness," "Grace's Window," and "Pillar of Cloud" have appeared in the "Living By the Word" column in *Christian Century* (December 1992–January 1993).

Scripture quotations are from the New Revised Standard Version of the Bible, © 1989 by the Division of Christian Education of the National Council of the Churches of Christ in the USA. Used by permission. All rights reserved.

Editor: Cynthia Shattuck
Copyeditor and Designer: Vicki Black
Cover Design: Vicki Black

This book is printed on recycled, acid-free paper and was produced in Canada.

Cowley Publications
28 Temple Place
Boston, Massachusetts 02111
1-800-225-1534

For
Trevor
Jack
Grace
Patrick

Contents

My Mother's Studio
Lent ◆ Season of Insight

Prayers in Sacred Time
Easter ◆ Season of Union

Homesick
Ascension ◆ Season of Unknowing

Pillar of Fire
Pentecost ◆ Season of Discipleship

Foreword

What is it that most people are hungry for today? What is it that they are seeking, seeking intensely with a deep desire? As I travel and meet many different people across all divides of denomination and place, it seems to me that in the end it is very simple: we search for a contemplative center for our lives.

This contemplative center is nothing abstract, theoretical, or cerebral. It begins where we are. In the end, it is all given. But we do have to open our eyes, unlock our ears, stretch out our hands, and be ready to receive what is already there. And often we need help with this. We need the encouragement of those who know the way because they have been there, those who can show us what we have and make it seem simple and accessible. And that is the beauty of this book.

As I picked up *Grace's Window* memories came to mind, vignettes of a friendship with Suzanne Guthrie stretching over many years: tea on the lawn under the shadow of an English cathedral; a walk along a cliff face with the Pacific Ocean roaring at our feet; the end of a service in a tiny chapel and a small child held warmly against the bright colors of eucharistic vestments; a pool deep in the woods with brilliant fall colors caught on its surface.

But other times and seasons came to mind too, when it was all not so glorious or so golden, times of shadows falling and words of pain. Books on prayer are worse than useless if they do not come out of the experience of the daily and relentless demands of ordinary life; out of trauma and desolation; above all, out of being alive to the world around. These are the essential threads that go into the making of the tapestry of this book. It is because there is not only light, joy, and wonder but also fear, loneliness, and darkness that the picture painted here is such a strong and convincing one.

When I started to read I found myself taken up and made part of a shared journey. For Suzanne, God is a God who moves, and that movement parallels the changes and the new life within her own self. So she shows a way that can never be static or easy or simplistic. She reminds us that a pilgrim comes to a holy place expecting to be changed. A pilgrim recognizes a holy landscape as a place mirrored within the soul. And it is not only the places of beauty that are creative. There are also the dark passages with desperate graffiti scrawled on the walls. So the book takes us on a journey which does not try to evade uncertainty, loss, and pain.

Suzanne also leads us on a journey through the liturgical year, as we go from Advent through Pentecost. Here the Christian year teaches us the mystical path of grace as each of these seasons evokes its own image, from conversion at the very start, through illumination and the dark night, to the fullness of the new shared life of Pentecost. I love this sense of rhythm, of relatedness to the elements, to the changes of the seasons, to being alive to time and place. Here is the gift of seeing, of curiosity, of intense observation of natural objects—without which, as Thomas Merton reminded us in *Contemplation in a World of Action*, the contemplative life becomes barren and routine.

To live this way makes demands, and asks for active cooperation on our part. There is nothing automatic about this kind of contemplative living. Wonder and the imagination need to be nourished and encouraged. The way of contemplative prayer is a way of discipline; it is hard work, and it asks for practice. Suzanne reminds us of something we need to hear again and again, that prayer is a kind of art, just as learning to play the flute is an art. When we practice this art, she tells us, it teaches us to "see and hear and perceive reality in new ways."

"Nothing in my life," she adds, "has been wasted as material for teaching me to pray." There is the most urgent message for the art of prayer in our own time. Gone is that terrible split between the material and the spiritual that so distorted the understanding of prayer in the past. Being holy, saying prayers, going to church: these took the whole idea of the holy and the spiritual away from the places in which we lived our lives, the tools we handled, the people we touched, the scenes we saw on the subway on the way to work.

Now we are once again rediscovering and recovering that wholistic spirituality which was a part of the earliest heritage of the church. Because it is life-giving, we need to listen to expressions of that spirituality from people like Suzanne Guthrie, whose voices we can hear because their lives touch ours, because they speak to us from a world we recognize and know as our own.

Esther de Waal

Prologue

One Saturday night someone pelted rocks through the east window of Santa Fe Mission in San Antonio, Texas. The next morning the priest and people arrived at the church to find the altar, pews, and floor covered with shards of stained glass. They boarded up the space behind the altar and from then on a series of hangings that changed with the seasons of the church year decorated the empty wall.

"That window made the church too hot anyway," the priest told me years later when I first came to Santa Fe. I asked the priest to tell me about each of the decorations, but instead of answering he asked, "Do the hangings mean something to you?"

They came to mean a great deal. Except for an elaborate Mexican tin cross for Christmas and Epiphany, and a colorful yarn *ojo de Dios*, "eye of God," for Pentecost, I thought they were ugly, but I loved them because they were loved by the people I loved. I particularly hated an old and sentimental portrait of Jesus that dominated the space in Lent until one Sunday I entered the church at the same time as an older man of whom I had always been a little afraid. "There he is," he whispered, and tears filled his eyes. After that, I saw the old man and the painting differently.

I learned to tell time by those hangings. Growing up in the Northeast I had always been able to tell winter, spring, summer, and fall by looking out the window. In San Antonio, with its banana trees and palm trees, an occasional freak ice storm at Thanksgiving but shirt sleeves on Christmas, I felt disoriented. I learned to tell the time of year by the scripture passages for the week and the priest on a ladder changing the seasons behind the altar.

Because my oldest son, Trevor, went to the nursery school in Santa Fe, I was able to pray in the church after I dropped him off and before I went to school myself in the mornings. After I prepared the altar for Sunday and marked the lessons for the readers in the huge Bible on the lectern, I read the lessons for each coming Sunday and began to feel through the scripture texts the rhythms and symbols and metaphors of the seasons in my prayers.

During the week at school, after my prayers in the empty church, I studied the classics of the Christian mystical tradition and the stages of prayer: conversion, the turning of all of your being toward the divine call; purgation, the lifelong, slow process of learning to pray; illumination, when the soul begins to perceive light and love; and union, the transformation of the soul. I learned about the transitional "nights" between the stages, which are perceived as abandonment because the soul cannot take in these intense concentrations of the reality of God, which "blind" it.

Soon I began to realize that the church year already reflected these mystical themes. The year's walk from anticipation to apostleship, from Advent to Pentecost, teaches us what to expect at each resting place; the seasons of the Christian year teach us to see that cycle of life and death mirrored in the seasons of our own soul.

Advent begins with the time-shattering apocalypse at the end of the world, reflected in our own soul when we first discover the need for God and turn in "conversion." At the darkest time of the year, Christmas teaches us to perceive the light penetrating the darkness, while Epiphany draws us to the light of Christ, gradually illuminating and transfiguring the soul in the "illuminative" way of prayer. Lent teaches us to love from the dark places of doubt and to persevere through this "purgation" even when the personal symbols and signs that first brought us to Christ fail. Easter turns everything upside down; all that is familiar is reconfigured, charged with God, as we experience the interconnectedness of all things in "union" with God. After the Ascension we might experience with the disciples a second desertion, a time of "unknowing" even more puzzling than the death on Good Friday, but in Pentecost we celebrate the love of the Holy Spirit and the call to go to the ends of the earth.

Because someone once smashed the east window at Santa Fe Mission and because the space was boarded up and replaced by symbols made of wood, straw, yarn, tin, and paint, I was given an ancient window into a way of understanding prayer.

◆

In 1979 my husband Pat and I, with our sons Trevor and Jack, moved to Fairfield, California, where Pat worked as a physician at the hospital on Travis Air Force Base. Our daughter Grace was born that year. I was ordained deacon and priest in 1984, going to work as assistant to the rector at St. Martin's Episcopal Church in Davis, and our youngest son, Patrick, was born between ordinations.

Every time I have moved, I have had to learn to pray all over again. The landscape of California presented me with new images to pray: the dry grass and circling hawks, the firestorms raging over the countryside in summer, the clouds tumbling off the coast and the heavy winter rains. Those years I felt I was tabernacled beneath a pillar of cloud and of fire. I watched the seasons in California as I read the scripture texts each Sunday, just as I had once watched the hangings change in the little church in Texas.

The forty meditations collected here reflect these particular places and times in my life, the hectic life of a military wife, mother of children, parish priest, driver of cars, and doer of errands. The thick, dusty tomes of prayer I read in seminary have never evoked for me the tears, anger, exhaustion, laughter, doubt, boredom, or deep joy I experience in prayer. I hope these meditations offer some idea of what it is like to enter the seasons of prayer through the window of grace God opens in a particular life.

GRACE'S WINDOW

Advent ♦ Season of Conversion

one
Praying the Apocalypse

All summer in Northern California the sun mercilessly bakes the earth, cracking it into jagged pieces, grasping life from every blade of grass. The hollow grass and dry earth and ominous breezes await the arbitrary whim of firestorms that rage over the countryside during the season after Pentecost.

I am afraid of California firestorms. One day while I was sitting on the floor sorting laundry, I heard the wind suddenly whip around the wrong corner of the house. Curious, I went outside to discover the sky over the hills blackening, and within a few minutes smoke completely covered the sun. As the sky darkened I saw the earth glowing, then erupt into flame as if just behind the hills the ground had opened up, collapsing piece by piece into a widening pit of hell.

I hurried the children into the car and then learned from the radio the fire was farther away than it seemed. A few blocks from us, police set up a barricade to prevent curiosity seekers from going toward the fire. We went home to watch the sky. I stayed alert all night after packing photo albums and other precious things in boxes near the door. The Napa Valley fire was contained eight miles from our neighborhood even though it had looked as if it were just at the end of our street.

In the late autumn in California, other portents appear in the sky heralding change. Clouds gather on the horizon. At sunset, blood-red rivers of light run between the last of this day's clouds. "Play outside now," say the mothers in our neighborhood. "Play outside as much as you can before the rains come."

By early December there is little daylight for play outside after school. Days are shorter; gray afternoons descend suddenly into blackness. Deep in the night, foggy moisture comes in low along the ground, across roofs and streets, between houses, pouring from the dark behind the streetlamp into the orange light.

Finally the rains come. The fire watch is curtailed but this is only a lull between dangers. The ground cannot hold the winter torrent of water that will come, and the flood watch begins. The portents in the sky in California inspire an unsettling and primitive fear in me.

Prayer arises out of the awareness of mortality, rather than the promise of eternal life. Praying begins not so much as a response to a secret, inner spiritual call, but rather to the worldly threat of change, personal cataclysm, or impending death. The soul recoils into a state of prayer. Prayer begins not so much in piety as in panic.

> *There will be signs in the sun, the moon, and the stars, and on the earth distress among nations confused by the roaring of the sea and the waves. People will faint from fear and foreboding of what is coming upon the world, for the powers of the heavens will be shaken. (Luke 21:25-26)*

The Christian year begins in late fall with warnings of the impending apocalypse. This chaotic upheaval reflected in its scripture readings in turn reflects the chaos of the individual soul in personal cataclysm. Just as individual prayer often begins in facing illness, death, change, tragedy, fires, and floods, the Christian year calls for conversion in the context of the end of the whole world, when the threat of apocalypse awakens the most radical call to prayer.

Perhaps every prayer in its essence is a cry uttered at the end of the world. Perhaps the end of the world bears every prayer ever murmured. Prayer occurs both inside and outside time. This summer's fire in California is the fire waiting the work of the winnowing fork. The flood to come this winter is Noah's flood.

Observing the sky at the onset of winter, I am almost afraid I have seen something I should not have seen. In blood-red sunsets and clouds lit with fiery wrath and beauty I have seen a rare secret, something terrible and beautiful. The end of time threatens upon the horizon, coming upon the clouds, but soon this vision closes in the dark cloud of winter. Soon the rains come.

During the rest of the time, during the other seasons, prayer does not seem so urgent. Still, I practice this prayer in Advent for that end time, that last crucial breath. I want to learn to pray so that my last moment might be prayer and not a hollow gasp. When I pray for God to rend the heavens and come down, when the skies open for the last time and the Son of man comes on clouds from the horizon, I want to look with longing, not fear, toward the horizon.

two
Aurora Borealis

Once in my childhood, I saw the sky open. My mother woke up the whole family and told us to put on our coats and come out on the front lawn. The sky blazed with luminous pictures. Moving lights like massive theater curtains billowed in a silent storm, suspended over us from somewhere deep in heaven. Random lights exploded like fireworks and confetti streamers. In the north a giant arc of all colors rippled in many directions at once, never losing its light, constantly changing but never moving.

I thought the stormy sky should have been as deafening as fireworks, because moving lights filled the sky from just above us as far into space as we could see and the move-ments were as wide as the horizons. But the aurora was silent. We would have slept through it but for my mother's wakeful eye.

She told me that Indians believed these giant northern lights were magical horsemen riding toward them bringing the end of the world. Did the horsemen bring doom or salvation? I don't remember. I could never imagine the Indians really being afraid of this sight, as awesome as it was; I sensed that such glory belonged to the sky. That night we simply beheld what is often there but hidden from our sleeping senses, like the silent presence of seraphim blazing amid the smoky train of God's mantle. That night we saw what is there but what we often cannot see.

When the northern lights faded we went inside. I spent another hour sitting on the floor, writing in my notebook with apostolic urgency about the experience, compelled to describe the indescribable.

In those days we lived outside the edge of town, where city lights did not obscure the night sky. As the town pushed its boundaries around us, it brought streetlights and the sky disappeared at night except for the barest outline of constellations. With such artificial light, we couldn't see the darkness—or know it, or learn about it, or come to love it. My mother never disapproved of my brother's battle of wits against the town. In a quiet act of vandalism he unscrewed the bulb of the streetlight in front of our house to give us back part of the night, but the town prevailed in the end. Even as a child I found it ironic that the artificial light of the streetlight was a world of darkness itself, veiling the magnificent lights of the night sky in a dull orange glow.

I have never seen the aurora borealis since. For whatever reason—city lights, streetlights, my own lack of awareness—there is never a dark enough night. But now I know it exists.

In California the night fog comes in slowly and then the rains come. The earth greedily quenches its thirst. The rains bring a new silence and peace in the spaces between the houses and in the streets.

Beware, keep alert; for you do not know when the time will come. (Mark 13:33)

The threatening clouds do not bring the end of the world and yet I have prayed the apocalypse. I have prayed the prayer of the dying. Prayer opened a new dimension of life for me, like a figure in a medieval book of hours lifting the flat blue backdrop of the sky at the horizon to peer beyond the firmament into a celestial realm of planets and stars. This prayer creates in me a desire to see and hear what is just behind my life, to look just beyond the streetlamp into the clarifying darkness, to listen for auroras in the silence, to try to express what is in the fantastic display just behind the darkness and silence.

If the apocalypse is at every moment, then I must pray at every moment. The urgency to pray is not only a call, but could become, perhaps, a way of life; a way of looking and then seeing what is there and what is meant to be seen, a way of listening and then hearing what is there and meant to be heard. Prayer becomes a way of transcending time and space, but at the same time it is a rediscovery of time and space, earth and sky, life and death, light and dark.

The watch upon the horizon is the waiting in darkness of uncreated light. Within the luminous night, you learn to see that the end of time undulates like aurora curtains at the boundary of the soul. Prayer teaches the whole of life to become a watch, for you never know when the sky will open its mysteries or when the Lord will come upon the blazing clouds.

three

The Music of Loneliness

Once, in the deepest part of the night, I heard the voice of my own loneliness. Except for the voice itself, I remember little else of the circumstances. I remember the cobblestones and white lamplight of Greenwich Village, and that I was with friends after a concert at a jazz club. We meandered through the Village, walking reluctantly toward the train that would take us back to Long Island. I was seventeen.

On a street I didn't know and would never find again, I heard the sound of a lone jazz saxophone. The player was invisible. No detectable movements came from doorways or basement stairs. The music filled the cavern above the narrow street, echoing as it might in a cathedral.

I remember thinking a banal thought: this could never happen in my neighborhood. Lights would come on, windows would open, people would shout, the phone in the offender's house would ring, the disturbance would be the talk of the school bus stop next morning. But here in the city, this sound of beauty and sadness, perfection and longing played upon one hundred windowsills in solitude.

We lingered on the street, listening. This cry in the night seemed to contain the essence of time itself. This music was not a rehearsal for another, more celebrated moment, nor a drill in technique and quality of sound, nor a recollection of some past triumph. This music belonged alone to this moment of solitude on this city street. This voice was a prayer rising to its god.

Suddenly it seemed, or seems in my memory, as though my own sadness and longing were outside myself and in the music. This unseen musician seemed to be reading my soul and playing it to the black and endless heaven. The music carried with it every inexpressible desire I could feel at seventeen and every longing I imagined I might ever feel. This sound taught me to recognize the cavern of emptiness within myself. Every possible seed of longing and sadness that lay hidden and untouched in my fate seemed to be put forth as an offering in the perfection of that voice in the night. Especially that unnamed and infinite longing that eclipses all others—the longing for God, rising to the unresponsive night, lost, unless the longing becomes a prayer.

I went toward the Long Island train with a new awareness, conceived in the musical notes of a stranger's prayerful sadness.

Afterward I would remember the music of my loneliness. My heart would refer to the prophetic sound of the saxophone as if it were the key to some ancient text of wisdom. I would recognize this voice at other times and in other forms, modulations, disguises, translations. I know this voice. It is persistent, it walks through dreams, it awakens me from sleep. It haunts the days, hiding in every shadow. I look for it even as I run from it, straining to listen even as I clap my hands to my ears like a child given a command she does not want to hear.

The voice clarifies a dilemma I would rather ignore, the dilemma of two equal fears: fearing God and fearing existence without God. If the foundation of existence is God, then everything about my life must change; if there is no God, no change is possible. My soul, like a deserted street, a wilderness of empty windows, hears the prophet's voice: if there is no God, there is no real loneliness, for if there is no God there is no such thing as real longing. And so the voice cries for me to turn every particle of my being toward the loneliness, to orient my life in a way that accommodates God's existence. I let in the invisible saxophone player to sing through my own soul, crying my heart aloud to the black sky, making my offering for me until I lift my own voice and make my cry of loneliness a prayer.

> *A voice says, "Cry out!" And I said, "What shall I cry?" All people are grass, their constancy is like the flower of the field. The grass withers, the flower fade, when the breath of the LORD blows upon it; surely the people are grass. The grass withers, the flower fades; but the word of our God will stand forever. (Isaiah 40:6-8)*

The prophet's exquisite cry is the forerunner to my first feeble lifting of my own solo voice in prayer. John the Baptist, the great teacher of prayer, cries aloud in the wilderness to prepare for the reality of the presence of God. I hear his voice as I turn in longing toward God and practice the conversion of my loneliness to prayer.

Is it possible that beyond the enfolding darkness the Lord cries out to me with longing?

four
Practice Time

> *Be patient, therefore, beloved, until the coming of the Lord. The farmer waits for the precious crop from the earth, being patient with it until it receives the early and late rains. (James 5:7)*

All autumn the strains of a saxophone playing "Jolly Old St. Nicholas," "Sleighbells Ring," and other holiday songs have come from the baby's room where my son practices. Practice time is in the early evening while I am cooking. I leave the kitchen stove to help.

"Try that measure with an F sharp. That's right. Now play the phrase."

Jack plays it correctly while I am in the room. Back at the stove and the over-browned meat, I listen. He renders the song with an F natural.

In the living room my daughter Grace plays an elementary version of the barcarole from *Tales of Hoffman* on the piano in 4/4 time despite yesterday's exhaustive coaching. I leave the kitchen and pull the opera from the record cabinet, find the aria, and draw my daughter to the record player.

"Let's dance it," I say. "*ONE* two *THREE ONE* two THREE ONE TWO THREE ONE two THREE ONE two THREE ONE two three ONE two three ONE TWO THREE!" We dance, our hands clasped together, smiling. We try it at the piano together. I return to the dried-out vegetables as the Barcarole mysteriously converts back into 4/4 time.

Upstairs there is a borrowed drumset whose music shakes the light fixtures. A wobbly, lurching anti-rhythm creates a surreal atmosphere. I go upstairs and stand in the doorway. Trevor finally looks up. There is a stunning silence.

"Why don't you practice with the metronome?" I suggest.

"It's too hard with the metronome."

"Precisely." I wait a moment and try again. "Do you want to see that program I taped with Max Roach teaching?"

"Not now, Mom. I'll just play along with the radio."

The rice has become crisp around the edges of the pan.

Prayer is an art that asks for daily attention. I found this discipline very difficult, especially at first. In many ways, learning to pray daily is like learning to play music. I think about this as I help my children learn to practice their instruments.

Learning to play music, like learning to pray, is a complex and tedious process that depends upon very boring rote work. Years go by before there is any real gratification. But the years of unrewarded labor at a musical instrument will ultimately yield music as well as the lesson of practice: in retrospect, all that time was a way of achieving disciplined progress toward any endeavor we undertake.

A friend describes prayer as playing a huge cathedral organ with myriad stops, swells, buttons, keyboards, and pedals that combine in infinite ways to make the music of prayer. This may be true, but if I thought of prayer as this complicated I would be afraid to begin. Every musician must start somewhere, if only by banging on a garbage-can lid or lifting the voice from speech into song.

The desire to pray beyond children's bedtime prayers, Sunday worship services, or cries to God for help can be paralyzing. To begin to pray can be a personal cataclysm, a radical shift of orientation. When I pray I am no longer autonomous. I am entering a larger world of which I am not in control. When I begin to pray under these circumstances I am confronted with the big theological questions: To whom am I praying? To whom or what do I address my prayer? "Dear God, if there is a God...." Does the world change when I pray? How do I know I am praying at all?

All over the world and from before history began, people have been praying. Yet I still stumble over the written music of the prayer book book and struggle with the rudiments of praise, petition, thanksgiving, intercession, and confession, all the while thinking about what I am saying, how I am saying it, my posture, my breathing, my concentration, my attitude, my motives, my integrity. Finally, it is simply praying that makes the difference: settling down in an atmosphere of relative quiet in a familiar place and at a regular time.

When I was a music student, a friend from India suggested that I approach practice time as a holy man approaches meditation. "Wash your hands and face, light incense or a candle, and then concentrate upon your practice as if it were a sacred ritual." The advice was good, and because I was romantic enough to be intrigued by it, these outward gestures of reverence enhanced the long hours. I found that I skipped less over passages that were difficult and that mastery over each stage of my practice seemed significant in itself. It was at first only a device for helping me concentrate, but I began to progress as I had not before.

I had stumbled upon the wisdom brought to light in the initial phase of mystical prayer: the "purgative way" of early Christian spirituality. In the beginning, a sacred time and place is crucial for concentration and discipline. The playing of each note is intrinsically good in itself. Tomorrow I will call upon each unconscious revelation that presented itself today, and what seemed like rote drilling will reveal itself as illumination. Only later will I realize all that boring time was sacred, and every yawned collect mumbled at night in the wing chair links me with the essence of humanity. Every gesture of reverence connects me to the cosmic battle between evil and good, true dark and true light, creation and the end of time.

My household saxophone player complains, *"Why* do I have to practice these scales? They're a waste of time. I already *know* all these notes!"

I tell him, "You have to practice scales to get a good, fluent sound, to read harder music faster, and to improve your breathing and your technique. Above all, you must know every scale and arpeggio, major and minor, plus a lot of other scales you haven't even heard of yet, so that you will be good enough to transform them into something new in case you ever start to improvise."

I want to tell him more. You must practice scales so that when the Spirit stirs up its power and comes upon you, you can play what it tells you uninhibited, unhindered by the clumsiness of your fingers or breathing or bad habits. Your sound must be so pure that you can translate the most divine secrets into a language other souls can understand, if God so wills it. You must prepare to be a servant to your scales now, so that later you will be able to play with more freedom than you can possibly imagine.

The beginning steps of mystical prayer are the scales and arpeggios, the studied practice, the beginner's years of patient labor.

At the school Christmas concert, the "Jolly Old St. Nicholas" wrestled with tearfully on the saxophone in the baby's room all autumn fills the gymnasium with the tunes of the other forty-five other children playing their part of the whole. Though it is a kind of purgatory to sit through, the school concert is also a glimpse of heaven. I am not the only parent swiftly wiping tears from my eyes in the darkened gym while straining to see three faces. One saxophone player seems to concentrate with only infrequent glances away from his music stand to search the darkened audience. Hidden in the percussion section behind the band, another face smiles beneath a thick shock of messy blond hair. I watch the gleaming triangle for the precise moment of his one note "solo." I thrill to the glimpse of a third face, almost lost between two bigger children on the wooden risers where the chorus stands—one tiny girl with an excited smile. The baby, lulled by the overwhelming noise of the band and chorus, nods to sleep in my lap.

In the dark before us, do angels weep with joy to hear our own laborious prayers?

five
Grace's Window

While cleaning my daughter Grace's room one morning I lifted the white eyelet bedspread and found two missing teacups from her toy china tea set. In each cup rested a tiny figure. Fra Angelico could not have painted a simpler or more transparent scene: in one cup stood an angel, arm raised, a herald of news, and in the other teacup Mary knelt in resignation and prayer.

I lifted the cups holding the miniature crèche figures as carefully as I could and put them on the nightstand, as if shaking them would dismantle the universe. For what I held in my hands was the pivot upon which salvation rests: Mary's delicate and uninformed yes, her unwavering assent that would mingle humanity's fate with God's love in a new way.

Then Mary said, "Here am I, the servant of the Lord; let it be with me according to your word." Then the angel departed from her. (Luke 1:38)

Could Mary have possibly known, anymore than I can know, what it means to carry and then to bear the Prince of Love? For Mary there was no incredulous questioning in the inner temple as Zechariah did, no wrestling match through the night by the River Jabbok like Jacob. She was struck neither dumb nor lame. Mary accepts an unseen, unborn, and unknown love. She proclaims, "My soul magnifies the Lord," as if she herself knew she would be a window of grace letting through the light of God's hidden love.

My prayers—those given to me by the church and its traditions as well as the spontaneous prayers of my heart—prepare my soul for this same moment, this same assent to a delicate thread of grace held before me. These are the prayers of listening, waiting, and receptivity.

Once a musician from New York came to coach some of the music students at my high school. When he heard my piece he said, "You play all right, but you don't play rests very well." I was puzzled, naturally, because rests are the moments or measures when you stop playing and wait.

We left the bandroom and he asked me to play my piece in the empty auditorium, which had better acoustics. "Now play, and listen to the silence between the notes. The silence between the notes is as important as the music itself."

Enhanced by the emptiness, the sound of my flute soared over the space and sang back from the far wall. But the silences where I paused to breathe were even more lovely and articulate, creating a wholeness I had not perceived before. The silence shaped itself to the voice of the flute. The loveliness of the music depended upon my saying yes to the silence between my notes.

In prayer, I am learning to observe the silences between the words. I am learning that I don't have to fill the empty space because the space will eventually sing for itself. The waiting and listening and silence teach, as slowly as the years of practicing do, that the active work of prayer must be balanced by the humble acceptance of grace.

In Advent, the prayers and hymns reflect the desire of the soul to accept this grace, this gift of love. We sing, "Let every heart prepare him room," and, "Let my soul, like Mary, be his earthly sanctuary." We pray, "May he find in us a mansion prepared for himself."

I must admit that I am afraid to say yes to the silences between my prayers. Even Mary was to lose her ecstatic vision when her son was born and her love for him was human, motherly. Perhaps I will not be struck dumb like Zechariah or lame like Jacob if I accept the love offered to me in a life of prayer, but I am not so foolish as to think I will not sometimes suffer.

To me, the dilemma of prayer in Advent is that if we accept the call of divine love, we also come face to face with evil. To be a person touched by God is to be engaged in the cosmic battle of apocalypse, the forces of good and evil drawn to the wide plain where we must fight or die. To turn in conversion is to calculate the cost and decide to go to the end in love, not with vague resignation but with the sharpened consciousness to which John the Baptist calls us.

Mary grieved beneath the cross with a broken heart. Although Jesus died for the world, love has not yet reached the ends of the earth. My own heart has its empty caverns.

Love waits behind the silence of prayer for my yes to a deepening capacity to love. Every love informs a greater love. Every lesser love is a forerunner of the great Love, sensed but never seen, to whom Mary once said yes.

In some mysterious way, Mary's decision to bear this love implies that I, too, can bear my loves. History separates us from that moment when God's love became incarnate and hidden in a child two thousand years ago, but sometimes grace opens a window. We are given the glimpse of a place, like the teacups hidden in the folds of Grace's bedspread, where the logic of our own world does not apply. Grace leaves us with the hope that in the silence of prayer somehow Love will mingle with our own feeble love and bring forth something new in us to give to those we love.

A SENSE OF PLACE

Christmas ◆ Season of Compassion

six

Rachel

At the final, frantic rehearsal for the Christmas Eve pageant in the church, as the children wait for final costume checks and entrance cues, I offer to help by distracting them from their mood of excited boredom. I love to hear these children talk about anything, so I decide to ask as many as I can what they think Christmas means.

The angels—fluttery girls from about age seven to eleven—answer angelically: "Peace on earth! Good will to all! Joy! Being happy! Sharing goodness!" They all share such radiant confidence about Christmas that I expect one of two of them to levitate or fly off into the ceiling's stained glass were they not thoughtfully holding one another's hands. The religious enthusiasm is so high that there are two Gabriels in the pageant this year—two girls whose hearts have been set since last Christmas on being the chief messenger of good news.

Since the angels are becoming unintelligible in their mutual giggling excitement, I go to the back of the church to help with the sheep and shepherds. The sheep are the littlest ones, from two to five years old, wearing headbands with cottonball ears. The shepherds are older boys from five to ten years old in striped tunics and bathrobe sashes and turbans. Compared to the angels, the shepherds are polite and relatively quiet. When I ask them about Christmas, they are more concrete and direct than the angels. They tell me Christmas is about the presents.

Soon it is time for the shepherds to meet the angels, who are increasingly fidgety and anxious to announce finally (the two Gabriels have been waiting a whole year!) the glad tidings of joy. Arms outstretched, each determined not to be the one whose arms tire first, the angels exultantly flutter down the aisle to meet the easily intimidated shepherds.

The Holy Family has been sitting patiently by the manger in front of the altar this whole time, watching everything. The blessed Lord Jesus in a pink bonnet sleeps in the manger box. Her natural mother waits beatifically in a front row nearby. Joseph, anticipating my question, flashes his swashbuckling smile: "Mom, if you're expecting me to come up with something good for your sermon tonight, forget it!"

Mary smiles.

This Mary is our youngest Christian. She is not the youngest child here, but even the sleeping infant in the manger is older in Christ than this pretty young girl named Rachel. I prepared Rachel for baptism and confirmation this fall, and she received her first Holy Communion on the Feast of St. Martin.

I had spent more time with Rachel than the other children who were preparing for confirmation simply because of her determination. She kept making appointments with me. I never said no, though I knew that Rachel would have some problem that was never a problem at all, but was what it seemed: an excuse to be with me. I visited her at her home, where we went for long walks down the alley behind her row of rented houses to a vacant lot strewn with broken bottles and discarded trash where her secret places were: a large pine tree, a hole in the ground with old tires to sit on, an abandoned barn that was condemned and dangerous. She told me about what she was thinking, or about her friends, or chattered on and on just to keep on talking. She showed me her new prayer book, the endpapers already filled with her own poetry and prayers.

In turn, I told her about the Rachel in the Bible: how Jacob loved her and had to work for her for seven years and then another seven, and how the covenant with Yahweh continued with Rachel as she bore Jacob's favorite two sons. I told her how Rachel hid the household gods from her father by putting them under a camel saddle and sitting on them pretending she didn't feel well "for the way of women was upon her," intimating to him that she had her period. This last bit of information was potentially scandalous not only to Laban, who fortunately went searching for his gods elsewhere, but to our own church school superintendent, who came to talk to me about the shocking things Rachel had picked up from her reading of the Bible. Like the biblical Rachel herself, I feigned ignorance and said I would talk to Rachel about it, inwardly resolving to be more careful with the superintendent in the future.

Despite Rachel's faux pas, the church school superintendent chose her to be Mary in the pageant. I approached the Mother of our Lord with my question about Christmas. She replied, "Jesus came to teach us what love is. He came to show us *how* to love."

Jesus came to show us how to love inside a world of broken glass and beer cans and old tires, within the junior-high gossip in the girl's room, despite the Sunday school superintendent's displeasure. Jesus began to teach us what love is inside the cruel cold of a cave full of animal noises and excrement, perhaps among other travelers and strangers, in the painful, bloody mess of birth. Meanwhile, nearby, the monotonous darkness tears open above a cold, rocky field. Stars are extinguished by other-worldly light, light from light, light behind light. Terrifying, strange beings pour out of heaven. Men and boys and sheep are utterly dazed, and sore afraid.

The sky closes. Darkness again. The frightened people must now bear the message of love. The shepherds stammer their praise.

But Mary treasured all these words and pondered them in her heart. (Luke 2:19) seven

A Sense of Place

*And the Word became flesh and lived among us, and we
have seen his glory, the glory as of a father's only son, full of
grace and truth. (John 1:14)*

According to the Christian mystical tradition, Christ dwells
in the human soul just as Jesus once dwelt in the flesh at a
particular time in history. It was possible to recognize the
man Jesus by his appearance, by the things he said, perhaps
by a particular scent, a laugh, a smile, a unique configura-
tion of teeth. Each human soul is also unique, even if Christ
dwells at the essence, because the soul inhabits a place.

Grounded in a sense of place, the soul's landscapes are
holy, whether rooted in the Sinai desert or Galilee, the Car-
pathian forests or Assisi, Benares or my backyard. From each
holy place canticles and symbols and metaphors emerge.
Every piece of holy ground shapes the destiny of the creature it nurtures. The metaphors of my soul are the landscapes known to me, and, in turn, my soul projects its own
insight onto things around me.

The places I have lived have always become dimensions of
my prayer. The desert wind in Texas reminded me of the
biblical image of the breath of God. The rains and
firestorms of northern California, evoking awe and fear, suggest the pillars of cloud and fire in the Sinai desert. My
childhood sense of place became the first ground for explor-
ing my soul.

The view from the east window of my second-story room
was part of the daily landscape of my soul as a child. There,
on my knees, my elbows resting on the window sill, I
watched and dreamed. From there I looked at a limitless ho-

rizon full of stars, at the luminous morning star, and at spectacular sunrises.

These experiences established the ground that yielded the image of Christ that eventually changed my life. The aurora's northern arc of light is to me the Son of man riding in on the clouds. The morning star is the same Star I sing of as I chant the Exultet beside the paschal candle at the Easter Vigil in the darkened church: "May Christ, the Morning Star who knows no setting, find it ever burning, he who gives his light to all creation...." I can no longer think of dawn apart from the words of Isaiah: "Arise, shine; for your light has come, and the glory of the Lord has risen upon you."

My family moved to the oak woods of rural Long Island when I was seven. The first interpreter of my new world was my mother. At first she was Adam in our backyard naming the night birds: "Listen! that's—a whippoorwill!" "That's—a quail." "That drumming sound is a grouse." "Listen carefully...an owl!" My mother was also my guide into the forbidding woods, showing me the first path I ever walked upon, a dry, sandy stream bed lined with trailing arbutus. "Lie down close to the flower and smell it." And in summer: "Watch that patch of milkweed. When it blooms it will be covered with monarch butterflies." "See that bump in the oak leaves? Look carefully under...no, don't pick them. They're rare! Indian pipes! See how they look like clay smoking pipes!"

I learned to measure time by the oak trees. Looking from my window over the woods just before spring, the tight buds formed a pink cloud beneath me, stretching to the horizon. As summer approached, the furry gray leaves emerged, extending fingers of pale yellow green. Later, dusty and dripping noisily with inchworms, full and shiny and very dark, the leaves smelled of sun and humidity. This very fullness of life in late September gave the foliage a heavy weariness. Suddenly the leaves were transfigured into variegated gold and orange and blood red, more splendid each year than I ever remembered before. Of all the trees, the oak clung longest to its leaves and finally faded, turning crisp and smooth and dull brown, dropping to the earth to cover once again the secret life in the ground. Then the naked limbs reached silently toward the charcoal sky as if in longing.

These were the seasons of my soul, teaching me to see some truth of time as it existed within myself. If I had not carried the capacity for change and new life within myself, I doubt I could have seen the constantly changing world of the oak woods. I would not have bothered to dig holes in the snow with my mittens to smell the ferment of decay that meant new life under the steamy veil of leaves over the ground. In the oak woods I discerned life beneath that which appeared to be dead. I awakened continually to the light of dawn and the cycles of sacred time.

Now, much later and far removed from that home, I think of the oak woods themselves as a metaphor for the landscape of my soul. The woods prepared my soul for infinite possibilities within the familiar and finite. The oak woods prepared me to accept mysteries that my intellect rejected for many years: that God dwelt in place and time in the Incarnation, and that the world beholds this glory. And that Christ, dwelling in my soul, will die and rise again.

eight
The Holy Name

I am attending a medical meeting in San Francisco with my husband after Christmas. Today the wives have been on a house tour and now the bus drops us off downtown for shopping at Macy's and Neiman Marcus. We admire the Christmas windows with scenes of a harlequin and his lady wearing elaborate black and white, gold and silver costumes set at a banquet, a balcony, a theater.

On the sidewalk between two display windows squats a shoeless woman in a filthy ragged coat with torn pockets, her possessions surrounding her in neat plastic bags. Nearby a musician plays fresh and majestic improvisations upon old jazz standards on his saxophone. His fingers ripple over the keys that he plays through woolen gloves with the fingertips cut open. I think to myself, "You'd pay a hefty cover charge in a club featuring big names to hear someone this good!" The shoppers, the shoeless woman, workers on lunch break listen to the music for the price of a few coins tossed into the saxophone case.

I don't know the name of the musician or the woman in the ragged coat, but suddenly I do know I can't go into Neiman Marcus and Macy's. I slip away from my group and lose myself in the afternoon crowd, revelling in the music.

More than at any other time of year, this season's call to reflection presents the extremes between happiness and loneliness, exhilaration and depression. Prayer heightens the awareness of joy and sorrow, peace and war, prosperity and poverty. This visceral prayer reminds me of early pregnancy, where those unnamed, unknown cells hidden deep within my body made me violently sick even before I knew I was pregnant. The hidden life of my children within me transformed my body chemistry so radically that for months all I could do was throw up.

To say yes to love is to accept a hidden life someplace in the darkness that is the Christmas of the soul. The incarnation of compassion begins in heart-sickness. Eventually the love is named.

A name is a holy place. The name is a womb that nourishes the one who bears it with all the love and hope mingled in the giving of the name. If not dictated by some angel, names are chosen carefully for saints or statesmen, prophets or poets, family doctors or relatives or places with wonderful sounds. Names are chosen with love in gratitude or by faith in potential or for hope of intercession. Names carry meanings within them, every year of life drawing out the meaning of the life of the named. Nicknames carry a seed of the grandeur of the name.

A child always hears his name. He learns to write it before he learns to write anything else. His name is posted on his pictures, displayed on the refrigerator, and carved into a wooden plaque over his bed. His name is on file at school with his phone number in case he is sick and must come home. His parents are re-named by his name: "Oh, there's baby Patrick's mother. Hi, Patrick's mother!" "Trevor and Jack's dad will take us to soccer practice today." "Grace's mom will bring the cupcakes to the school party." The rhythm of the rocking chair conforms to the name chanted in the darkness.

Patrick's house! Patrick's shoes! Patrick's new coat! Here are Grace's doll, Grace's window, Grace's teacups. Jack's name is sought eagerly among the names of the beginning band students on my Christmas concert program. His name is underlined and the program is placed carefully in his file with old report cards, certificates, pictures and drawings, letters, playbills and ticket stubs. Names appear upon the flyleafs of important books: "To Trevor on his first day of school, fifth grade. To help inspire your many discoveries, with love from Mommy and Daddy, August 29, 1984."

Daily the name becomes more holy, said thousands of times in thousands of ways as the child grows and is checked by discipline, chastised, guided, given gifts with the letters of the name written on a tag. The names are prayers whispered in the night while tucking goosepimpled legs into warm blankets. The holy names preside over the greetings and the goodbyes and upon letters over a lifetime. The names are worked together like worry-beads, spoken through the nights of absence.

These holy names are familiar resting places upon a path of light. But even Buddha in his garden palace, carefully protected from the world, could not escape forever from the sight of the nameless, calling him to the sickness of heart that is compassion. Compassion drove the Buddha to leave his palace of light and love to seek the dark paths of godly wandering in the unknown, for he knew then that truth confined to the way of light alone is only half a truth. Sooner or later, by the glow of light emanating from the beloved, you see in the shadows the contrasting figures of the unloved, watching. How can you pray the familiar words of the children illumined by the light of your own love without fumbling to form words for those with names unknown watching from the darkness?

Herod, seeking a child with a holy name, killed all the wrong children. Even now, nothing has changed. Even as I love my children day and night, and simply because I love them, I am aware of others unloved and unknown who seem capriciously born in the wrong place with the wrong name.

Where are You among those without a dream, with no angel to warn them, no place to flee?

Love is the most fragile of all blessings and the most anguished of all prayers. I know that I love only because I am loved. Love is conceived by love and love is nourished by love. A name is nothing but an empty word unless it is infused with love.

> *After eight days had passed, it was time to circumcise the child; and he was called Jesus, the name given by the angel before he was conceived in the womb. (Luke 2:21)*

The shoeless woman and the saxophone player bear witness to the nameless. The gulf between the named and the nameless will remain until all of us are called by the holy name, which is love.

nine

The Pilgrims' Way

The view from Grace's window is the most beautiful in the house, for it looks out upon hills and a horse pasture and a neighbor's backyard trees. The clouds and rain have drawn out the hidden life behind the dead grass on the hills, first gray and then, almost overnight, a deep and velvet green for Christmas. The holy cloud awakens life within charred seeds that flourish all the more for the layer of fertile wet ash over the earth. Winter rains that seemed ominous have proved fruitful; clouds that seemed to herald the end of the world have brought new life.

The secret weaving of faith in the soul occurs in the deepest part of the night. Fog coming in from the ocean in the dark, bringing cool and life-giving rain to the hills, is like the hidden divine presence coming into the soul. The roots of faith strengthen and swell unseen, woven into an intricate network deep in the darkness of the soul. Prayer is largely unconscious and hidden. Once you begin to pray, prayer becomes a life deeply hidden within, rooting itself in the darkness. I pray when I do not know that I am praying.

I remember wondering why I would find myself weeping in church long before I believed in anything. My struggle at the time was that I did not want to believe something that was not true, because if it were true, I knew I would have to give the whole of my life for it. Wishing something is true does not make it true. I think, in retrospect, I cried in church because something had already taken root in my soul. There was something to respond to although I was not yet aware of it—a life of prayer already deeply rooted in my desire for truth. The desire for truth meant rejecting "God" and religion as I knew it. The desire for truth meant being rootless and without faith for a cleansing period of time. It led me back to the threshold of belief in God, which seemed at the time like the end of the world.

> *How dear to me is your dwelling,*
> *O LORD of hosts!*
> *My soul has a desire and longing*
> *for the courts of the Lord;*
> *my heart and my flesh rejoice*
> *in the living God. (Psalm 84:1)*

When a child is on the threshold of a developmental stage she behaves nearly intolerably. Just before she learns to crawl, just before she learns to walk, and especially just before she learns to talk, she rages with the frustration of wanting the achievement at hand but fearing the inexorable change that achievement will mean. Families complain of the "terrible twos," but any experienced parent can, at the same time, watch with reverence the thrilling changes about to take place in their child at any age.

The child crawls, pulls herself up, finally walks and quickly runs. She explores each phase of her expanding world eagerly, with curiosity, energy, joy, even passion. Sometimes she is so busy learning she falls asleep in the act of climbing or eating or playing because the urge to learn is so compulsive and exhausting. Up until now she needed only to cry to get her milk, to have her diaper changed, to receive comfort. She plays a game of sounds until she perceives the sounds have meaning, when the Eden of babyhood ends with the responsibility of language. The complexity of her world demands more than food and comfort. She wants a certain stuffed animal in her bed, she wants her oldest brother to come to her, and sometimes she has some nameless desire beyond her own understanding—she wants the meaning behind the sound. You say, "What do you want?" and if she could talk she would cry, "I don't know!" So she just cries.

The terrible twos prefigure the same developmental dynamics encountered in adolescence but also anticipate stages in the spiritual life. What do you want? asks an inner voice. And you cry and cry, "I don't know! I know it's *something*, but I don't know what it is!"

Suddenly and finally, the child becomes completely articulate. Her thoughts are shaped by subject and predicate and the limitations of her vocabulary, and never again does she hear or see as she did as an infant. From now on she thinks in words rather than in senses. The two-year-old rebellion ends. She has forgotten her frustration and fear and fascination. There is peace at home.

In prayer, too, peace comes. Until it is time to grow in God again.

I see myself in the last row of a church, detached, coldly skeptical of the liturgy, the choreography of faith, unfolding before me. Through the years I journey up through the nave, row by row, year by year, church by church, sometimes on Sunday, sometimes alone during the week, pacing, fidgeting, storming out forever only to return again. I fight the battles of canonical belief with teachers and priests, fiercely determined to seek truth whatever the outcome. I keep notes of my progress as if I am unwinding a string in a cave, so that if I get too far into a silly, convoluted Christian faith, I can find my way out again. During an Advent lasting over a decade, I journeyed as far as the chancel, finally kneeling with taut back, in a posture grasping for perfection, the altar rail stained with the sweat of forearms and irrational tears. "What do you want?" I don't know.

Eventually, the sounds of the empty church where I prayed alone—the rhythm of cars on the road outside, the chattering of sparrows in their nests in the ivy under the eves, the creak of roof and whisper of rain—became so familiar that one day, without thinking, I pulled myself into a new dwelling place inside the chancel, stretching out my feet on the warm rug, resting my head lovingly in the elbow of the inside corner of the communion rail.

Watching the east wall above the altar, I listen to the silence between my breathing, entering the blazing darkness behind the beating of my heart.

The sparrow has found her a house
*   and the swallow a nest where she may lay her young;*
by the side of your altars, O LORD of hosts,
*   my King and my God.*
Happy are they who dwell in your house!
*   they will always be praising you.*
Happy are the people whose strength is in you!
*   whose hearts are set on the pilgrims' way. (Psalm 84:3-4)*

STARGAZERS

Epiphany ◆ Season of Illumination

ten

Stargazers

In a partitioned room off the nursery school in a barrio
church in San Antonio, a small group of women decided to
meet every Wednesday morning. We were all housewives
with little children who had dedicated our busy lives to
prayer. Together we wrote a rule of life, choosing a six-
teenth-century saint, Angela, as our patron. St. Angela had
established a rule of life for women living with their families
at home and doing catechetical work in their own neighbor-
hoods. Realizing that the usual mechanisms of social change
(government, politics, church hierarchy) could do very little
to make people's lives better in a chaotic and corrupt state,
she reasoned that true social change would come about
through the education of young girls who, as educated
young mothers, could in turn influence generations through
rearing their children with love.

My youngest son, Jack, and the other smallest children
played in the nursery room with a babysitter we hired for
two hours every week. My son Trevor and another woman's
children attended the church's preschool on the other side
of the partition. As we studied together we could hear our
children sing, recite their ABCs, and play. The kitchen behind us smelled of cumin, cilantro, rice, and beans cooking
for the children's snack. Occasionally, the rooster next door
crowed.

In addition to the Bible, we studied books we kept in a
cardboard Texas Ruby Red grapefruit box: books by Teresa
of Avila, Francis of Assisi, Augustine, Thomas Merton,
Thomas à Kempis, Francis de Sales, Thérèse of Lisieux. We
talked over our rule every week, discussing our daily individual goals, accomplishments, failures. Magdelena told us how

prayer came to interrupt her soap opera in the afternoon. Grace shared secret and sometimes funny messages through scripture citations we had to look up. Veronica brought tapes of popular love songs and interpreted the music in ways that seemed to express our intuitions as women of prayer. Diana made comic presentations about the difficulties of finding time for prayer and quiet as a military wife and mother of four children. Leslie struggled to express larger community issues within the context of our little partitioned room. We teased, laughed often, cried, confessed our weaknesses, and encouraged each other in our lives of prayer on Wednesday mornings and during the week over the telephone.

Our rule combined four elements: prayer, study, work, and mission. These elements were fluid, each part of the rule nurturing the other parts. Diana called it "the square rule" and drew a picture of concentric boxes with "prayer" at the center surrounding our relationship with God, and "mission" on the outside extending to "the ends of the earth."

The heart of our rule was prayer. Silent prayer and contemplation could teach us awareness of our connectedness to the Divine Presence. The practice of daily disciplines of prayer and corporate worship could sanctify time and connect us to the church and to each other. Scripture and holy reading, done daily, nourished our prayer, work, mission, and the whole of our lives. Taking inspiration from the Shakers, who said, "Put your hands to work and your hearts to God," and St. Teresa, for whom "God moves amongst the pots and pans," we talked about the spirituality of our daily work. We read Brother Lawrence, who found that even so much as lifting a piece of straw off the kitchen floor could be a profound experience if accomplished for God. We talked to each other about our lives in the context of prayer and the love of God.

Each of us had specific "missions" we assigned ourselves that represented our service to our neighbor, even if it was simply making an extra phone call each day. This had to be some kindness or confrontation or witness we would not normally have done without our accountability to our rule and to each other.

In retrospect, I see that these Wednesday mornings were among the happiest times in my life. Because of them my house became a cathedral in which I learned to pray under every circumstance. Living a rule with others began to give me habits of compassion, gratitude, virtue, and inner joy.

The women's movement had not yet influenced us. For a few of us, church was the only activity our husbands "let" us participate in, presumably because church was "safe." But the Holy Spirit is the most subversive of all movements. St. Paul, quoting Isaiah, proclaims:

> *For it is written, "I will destroy the wisdom of the wise, and the discernment of the discerning I will thwart." Where is the one who is wise?...Has not God made foolish the wisdom of the world? (1 Corinthians 1:19-20)*

Veronica, Grace, Leslie, Magdelena, Diana, and some of the other housewives who came from time to time certainly were considered foolish and even worthless—by themselves as well as others. But I knew as we studied our texts and poured over the charts and maps of the spiritual life set before us through the writings of holy teachers that I sat with wise women, with magi.

After St. Angela's death the medieval church quickly forced the remaining women to accept enclosure, monastic habits, and traditional vows, so that this powerful lay movement could be more easily controlled by the hierarchy. This fact was not lost on us. Our school of prayer became for some of us the beginning of our radicalization as Christians in the church. For each of us, the time came when the star rose in the East and we knew we had to go and follow, at whatever cost.

How did the magi know to follow the star rising in the East? Perhaps the wise men followed the star after a lifetime of watching—scanning the sky, reading the movements of the stars, tracking the paths of constellations and the courses of planets. Maybe they collected chests full of maps and charts of earth and sea and sky. They knew from ancient and esoteric books that a particular new star would announce the birth of a Messiah. After a lifetime of preparing themselves with the study of wisdom, of meditation and prayer, with interpreting dreams and visions and watching the sky, the magi perceived the dawn of a holy light. Consulting with one another, they recognized what it was, and what to do, and when and where to go.

I want to live my life like the magi. I want to perceive the movement of divine light upon the horizon. I want to live a dedicated life, so that even for one moment in my life I, too, may see the glory of the Lord face to face.

eleven
First Love

Rain clattered against the wooden roof, diminishing at times only to dramatize the impact of the next onslaught. All the excitement of the night was outside, running along the roof, sliding down the noisy gutter pipes. Bursts of rain scattered reflections from the street lamp into hundreds of gyrating puddles of orange light along the parking lot.

Inside the parish conference room, the late hour, the faint hum of fluorescent light, and the carefully worded arguments had made a dull meeting duller. When it ended, the adults dallied by the coffee machine to talk, as if the meeting had not been long enough. Two teenagers slipped outside to wait for their ride home.

A loud crack against the roof announced another downpour. Someone opened the sliding door and called out to the boy and girl sitting on the fence rail. "Kids! Come in. You'll get soaked. You'll catch cold."

The girl, torn between the sensible advice of the adults and the intrigue of the moment, looked to the boy for a signal. He took her hand. They would wait in the rain.

Time passed and the rain did not abate. Someone else with more authority pulled aside the sliding door and called to them again, but it was pointless. Sitting together on the fence in the torrent of rain, their warm hands clasped together, droplets falling off loose hair, streams of water running in cool rivulets inside their coats and down their skin, they were more intensely alive at that moment than any of us.

The rain became gentle again and after a time the couple came up to the porch to collect their belongings: his saxophone case, her flute, their school book bags. Just then the boy's mother pulled up in the car. By way of greeting she called to me distractedly, "What a storm! See how wet the children have got from the porch to the car!" And she drove off.

What do you expect? I thought. They have just been baptized.

During the following weeks I saw or imagined that I saw a change in the young woman. Her charm and grace and carriage betrayed an inner transformation that those closest to her could not notice. Drawn out of the small circle of friends and family, she had entered a larger world irrevocably changed by longing and longing transformed, her soul awash with love as if the heavens opened for her alone. Henceforth her hidden desire will be to love with all her heart and with all her mind and with all her soul and with all her strength. She was created for love.

The one who is more powerful than I is coming after me; I am not worthy to stoop down and untie the thong of his sandals. I have baptized you with water; but he will baptize you with the Holy Spirit. (Mark 1:7-8)

How like the awakening to a life of prayer is the awakening to a life of love! She prays her lover's name, recites slowly to herself the sacred texts of his letters, and sings the canticles of his praises to her. She meditates upon his voice, his hands, his face. The fence rail where they held hands the first time becomes a sacred place. She comes here as if on pilgrimage to remember the moment her soul began to open to the Other.

Through this icon of love, this pale, thin boy, she has caught a glimpse of the Infinite behind the finite, the Creator behind the created, the ineffable behind the sensual, the uncreated light illuminating the icon itself. A small flame has begun to lick the edges of her own soul.

Perhaps from now on she will pursue that glint of the Blessed One under every aspect of creation. Because she has seen it once when the heavens opened, she will look for it again in every aspect of her life: in work and chores and school, in people and books and places, in art and music and thought. Perhaps she will learn to recognize that divine spark which may reveal Love behind what she sees, transfixed for a moment in the intersection of sign and grace called sacrament. She will want to drown herself in sacrament.

Well-meaning or jealous friends and relations may convince her to turn away from her first love, to come in out of the rain. She is too young, they may say, for her to love with this intensity. Perhaps from then on she will hide her passion or search for it elsewhere. Those of us who observe her will either find ourselves unaccountably happy at the couple's parting of ways or vicariously saddened not to see this romantic love continue.

And what of the lover? His voice calls her, singing to her of new life, wooing her soul into awareness, leading her by the hand, however inadvertently, to the threshold of the inner journey. By a word or two he could quench the new flame within her, but he does not. He holds off the world for a little while so that the light can grow strong. Still, he will not allow himself to be mistaken for the Bridegroom; he is the forerunner to a brighter flame. Together they were baptized into love upon a fence rail in a rainstorm; later, she will be baptized by fire in the love of One mightier than he. Neither one thinks of love in this way—they are simply two kids in love.

Much later, when her prayer is as impassioned as new love, she will think about this first love in a different way. This boy will dwell in her memory as the herald of her soul's awakening, a burning and a shining lamp giving light to her light. Like the heavens opening and the spirit descending in baptism, love confers a new and irrevocable wisdom upon the human soul. Love can baptize the soul into divine love. In this way, a young girl's first love is to her the greatest of all prophets.

twelve

Come and See

When Trevor was very little he often wanted to look at a box where I kept my earrings and a necklace. It was not the jewelry he was interested in, but a tiny starfish, a shell, and a piece of petrified wood. These objects were souvenirs of a childhood spent in intense observation of the natural world; they had somehow survived the continual culling of childhood things through moves and marriage. The starfish, shell, and petrified wood had survived my growing up.

I was very harried as a young mother, but even so I don't understand how I could have been so impatient with Trevor over the jewelry box. My own childhood was inquisitive and marked by hoarding, my drawers filled with birds' nests, sea anenomes, mussel shells, arrowheads, rocks, and fossils. My bookcase was crowded with horseshoe crab shells, jars of polliwogs, seaweed specimens, and dried flowers. The dresser top displayed roots, leaf cuttings, seeds, and feathers. One year I carried a "soil sample" around in my Sunday coat pocket.

I never remember my mother objecting to this collection of flora and fauna and artifacts. Her own pockets also had mysterious bulges. I remember her peering at something with her one myopic eye, lifting her thick glasses over her forehead to look closer, or deftly grabbing the binoculars always at hand in the kitchen window to focus on some movement in the oak trees. Once, watching the clouds at sunset, I heard her remark, "If anyone painted that color no one would believe it."

When supper dishes were done my mother always spread some project out on the kitchen table. My earliest memory of the mysterious time after my bedtime is of enticement to come downstairs because there was always something to see. It took her four years to build a ship model of *The Golden Hind*, intricately painted, rigged with tiny ropes and pulleys.

On Saturdays after the grocery shopping was done my mother took us to the library. The more efficient the shopping, the more time we had at the library. From the time I can remember, the Guthrie children were never confined to the children's room; my mother left us on our own while she looked for a week's worth of books for herself. The books my mother found were always unusual and appealing sitting on our coffee table all week—she was interested in travel, history, ships, art, biography, literature, and science. Sometimes I would nonchalantly follow her to try to find out the way she discovered her books. I often wondered how she found treasures on the same library shelves my brother and sister and I had seen but missed somehow. She simply saw more than most people do.

Because I was the youngest I was home from school first in the afternoons. I could find my mother in her tiny studio sitting at her drafting board in a posture not unlike a little girl, her long legs tucked between the rungs of the high stool. If she was not finished with whatever she was working on that day, I would be allowed to stay nearby. Sometimes she would let me play with her artist's mannequin, a wooden human figure like a doll without a face that bent at the joints, or the eerie gray foam hand with veins and muscles and fingernails that you could bend into any normal hand movement. I remember trying to shred kneaded erasers or arrange the paintbrushes, each possessing a unique tactile magic. The studio smelled of turpentine, ink, and oil paint.

Often my mother would give me paper and charcoal pencils or india ink to work with. Looking at my stilted and unimaginative attempts to copy something, she would say, "Draw what you see, not what you think you see."

My mother's own passion for truth, for drawing what she really saw, not what she thought she saw, extended to life. I could not draw exceptionally well, and I knew I did not have the passion for drawing that she did. But I heard her message: be aware of truth, not what you think is truth.

My mother was not a religious person, although she sent us to church because, she reasoned, we couldn't intelligently reject religion unless we had exposure to it. She herself could not accept formal religion. "Theology is built upon unwarranted assumptions," she used to say. She could not believe in something that might not be true. It was, however, her very discipline and passion for truth that gave me the foundation for a life of passion for God. In this way my mother was my most fundamental religious influence. Not that she intended it that way, or even approved. But one truth leads to another.

My mother taught me to *see* through her painting, her love of books. She taught me to see on August nights, lying on the army blanket watching meteor showers and pointing out constellations. She taught me to see on sudden trips to New York City museums that were not for the sake of our "education" but rather because of some private compulsion to see a particular exhibit and her delight in having us go with her.

> When Jesus turned and saw them following, he said to them, "What are you looking for?" They said to him, "Rabbi" (which translated means Teacher), "where are you staying?" He said to them, "Come and see." (John 1:38-39)

Curiosity brought the disciples to Jesus. Curiosity is the foundation of true education, the love of life, of prayer. Come and see the unfolding of what is new in every moment, the uncovering of layer after layer of reality, of love, of light. Pray as you are drawn to pray, not as someone has told you how to pray. The ancient "illuminative way" of prayer is seeing the extraordinary reality of God in the ordinary, detecting the movement of the sacred within the mundane. Gather all that you see outside yourself and bring it in to see up close, to magnify the Lord, to see God blazing behind the starfish, the shell, the petrified wood.

thirteen

Morning Prayers

Glorify the Lord, O nights and days
O shining light and enfolding dark.
(A Song of Creation, BCP 88)

Called out of sleep by the foraging grunts and clucks of my infant child and by the discomfort of full breasts, I hastily change his diaper before his hunger wails are audible to anyone else. It is too early for the others to wake up, and I want this time to be spent in solitude.

The room is blanketed in shadows and I am warm with the child close to me, the gray wool shawl around my head and arms like a tallith. I nursed my four babies in this predawn hour by the east window, with the light of the morning star illuminating my breast and the child's head. Although I was always too exhausted for deliberate prayer, in retrospect I believe those hours must have been times of deep prayer—prayer in silence, as if dwelling with the Word before words; prayer in the darkness, as if within the one uncreated Light before light.

The star fades and then disappears with the dawn, daylight exposing the room's dusty books and files, piles of mending, letters. Confronted with things left undone, and the noises from the kitchen of other children searching for food (non-nourishing, no doubt), I am summoned to the things to be done in a hurry. It is as if creation was fashioned *into* chaos instead of *out of* chaos, when God separated the light from the darkness with the ordering of time. As if, after that first and holy morning, came the sudden span of earthly time: human history as it is presented on a social studies test, abbreviated and superficial, facts and dates memorized but not learned. So cluttered with detail and movement in the urgency of cooking breakfast, getting ready to go to work, and dressing children unwilling to go to school and insisting they do not hide their shoes on purpose. The predawn hour is like a primal memory: hidden, forgotten, cloistered in some holy enclosure of the soul.

"Open my lips, O Lord, and my mouth shall proclaim your praise," I say aloud in the daily office, but more likely my lips will open to settle disputes or to give directions, blame, requests to hurry up. It is hard to imagine I once rocked the older ones quietly in predawn light, for these children of the morning, anything but contemplative, are more like spinning electrons on an untouchable axis in irregular and sometimes colliding orbits. The oldest helpfully dresses the youngest while the middle two panic in a crisis of missing books and shoes.

The children are in the car before I brush my teeth at last with only a quick glance in the mirror. Time has fastened its impression too fast on my skin, which looks more each day like a sheet of thin rumpled tissue paper. The fine acoustics of the garage accentuate the car horn calling for me over and over as I brush my teeth. I am late, and Trevor has a math time-test at eight o'clock. Yet, surprisingly, I perceive that this is the sacred moment. I am full of God, and must God come to me when I'm brushing my teeth but not at prayer? Or is that the point?

The demands of life lived in time invade my prayer—or is it that prayer invades daily time? I spit and rinse and wipe and grab my keys and purse and letters to mail and run out the door. "Worship the Lord in the beauty of holiness. Come, let us adore him."

The divine office, the daily saying of morning and evening prayer, teaches me to perceive holy time behind ordinary time. Not only the rush of God while brushing my teeth, but the living of every moment is sacred. The music of the spheres, the planets whirring on their taut gravitational strings journeying round the sun, is implicit in the whirling dervishness of the children and in the daily circuit of obligations and errands. The saying of daily prayers is a way of learning to tell time not only in recognizable moments of grace but within the daily struggles to stay on time.

Even though my formal prayers are said in the wing chair or in the cold midweek church, the effect of them opens the day to things I would not see if I hadn't prayed. From the mailbox at the end of the driveway I see the heavy layer of Bay Area fog resting behind the mountains, and a thick, white arm of cloud embraces the two peaks of Twin Sisters. In the morning the cloud is the theophany of Yahweh on Mt. Sinai. In the evening the fog is the theophany surrounding Jesus on Mt. Carmel.

The car horn, frantic with the impending math test, summons me from theophany to cacophony. I slam the letters into the box and off we rush to the schools and babysitter and then to work.

I make the same circumscribed patterns over Fairfield and then to Davis each day. I perceive in my own monotonous travels that there is a purpose to it even if, like the Israelites in the Sinai desert, I go in circles for forty years. The long commute on Highway 80 between Fairfield and Davis is transformed with each passage into holy ground. The journey itself gradually reveals a sacredness as compelling as the destination. Like the lines on my face, the experience of the journey itself deepens my life and leaves its mark. The more time I spend wandering in Galilee, or in the Sinai desert, or driving around Fairfield, the more I learn to see.

fourteen
Noon Office

Rejoice always, pray without ceasing, give thanks in all circumstances. (1 Thessalonians 5:28)

My work at St. Martin's is as distracted as my prayer, as chaotic as my mornings getting four children out of the house by 7:30. My daily task is to render an art out of interruptions, to pull onto one canvas the drab colors of broken time that are in pieces like an off-centered cubist painting, and to make it whole and balanced. I rush about all day knowing what I want to accomplish by two o'clock but without always anticipating the daily obstacles.

Most of my office work takes place at a makeshift desk in a corner as unpretentious as a watercloset. This particular ministry is not a difficult job. The day is filled with too many pleasant people. I give too much attention to too many things at once while receiving too much thanks for doing too little.

As busy as I am, I don't feel particularly useful. It is not as though I am a builder of houses for refugees or a digger of wells or a distributor of medicine or clothing or tools. I have never given relief or counsel in the name of God on the battlefield or in a natural disaster. I do not find housing for the poor or fight for fair laws to protect the oppressed. In this suburban university town we proclaim the gospel with type-writer and telephone, newsletter, Sunday bulletin, and the church calendar of events of the month. As at home, there is the maintenance of the building, the calling and waiting for the repairman or plumber, the man to change the locks to protect the photocopy machines that are the tabernacles of God's incarnation here. This work is less like the apostles' preaching than answering complaint mail for a department store.

I pray with the sick, help a few people with a little time on their hands to love scripture through studying together, and preach polite sermons to the already converted. I do no less and no more than what any Christian neighbor would do. I figure they pay me for this because everyone is so busy there is not enough time for us to be neighbors to one another, so we pitch in and get an ordained person to be the Christian neighbor.

Like a good priest, I live the same life as the people I serve. I am the busy mother and wife, running in circles and never accomplishing anything. My children, with piano lessons, saxophone lessons, soccer, swimming, and scouts, are over-busy with activities to which I drive them in the car every day after school.

The families in my parish live the same way. Church activities are another "thing" to schedule into a crammed calendar. We come to church neither for solace nor for strength, neither for comfort nor renewal; we come anticipating the next thing we will have to do after church. The over-stimulated youth will attend youth group meetings if the activity is as amusing as the other activities that engage their limited time. I don't blame them. A woman in my parish describes our kind of life as being like a "water bug frantically darting across the top of the pond, never able to stop or drink deeply of the beauty of life."

Something deeply sinful lies at the root of this way of living, but I am simply too busy to think about it. I can't seem to step out of the relentless circles of suburban family life. Somehow, we and the people with whom we share this life agree that something is wrong and leave it at that, because we have determined this is the best way to raise our children.

I don't want to do this kind of ministry the rest of my life because I can't imagine living at this hectic pace myself for very long, as pleasant as it is in many ways. But I think about men and women who live in daily danger, who do heroic works, who exhaust themselves for God. Perhaps I, too, will be called to be heroic someday, to drop immediately what I am doing to live a more radical life in Christ. In the meantime I rush around within these small circles of modest discipleship with what I hope is faithfulness.

Maybe the disciples felt the same way on their long walks up and down Galilee from village to village, through Samaria to Jerusalem for festivals and back again. There must have been a lot of walking.

For now, this is the work of God in the church, and like the work of God in the daily office, it is not a matter of individual heroics but the blending of one voice into a vast chorus. These are not my prayers, after all, but a part of a great human prayer of daily struggle to see God and to do the work of the kingdom in the world. As I reflect upon the past day at work on the way home, which has been pleasant and mundane but still mysteriously tiring, I wonder if in a sense I am praying continually, as Paul encouraged the congregation at Thessalonica to do. Even if I were a nun, I would have to brush my teeth and mail letters and answer the telephone and learn to perceive each phone call as a call from our Lord and not another silly interruption.

Observation sustains prayer. Prayer, like an art, trains the person of faith to perceive in this heightened sense the holy

---

behind the ordinary. And if deeper prayer invades, it is through God's grace and not because of the extremes of my cold piety or fervent devotion. Like a manual on aesthetics, the prayer book offices give me an overall scheme in which to interpret the pieces of relentless interruptions and fragmentations of suburban busyness—even as far removed from ancient Israel as California is in the 1990s. Without plodding through the prayer book offices regularly, I would not learn to watch for God's creation in the morning or reconcile myself to the day's work or watch and hallow what I find when evening comes.

fifteen
Wing Chair

Now as we come to the setting of the sun,
and our eyes behold the vesper light,
we sing your praises, O God. (Phos Hilaron, BCP 118)

Light begins to fade. The sunsets I may or may not notice. I am driving someone somewhere or cooking dinner or bathing somebody, and the vesper light may be the fluorescent light of kitchen or bathroom. The news on the radio filling the house with the world outside competes with the hissing of the smoking, overheated frying pan—it is getting late and I try to compensate with heat what I have lost in time.

"Let my prayer be set forth in your sight as incense, the lifting up of my hands as the evening sacrifice." We eat in haste. Pat or the older boys must rush to a meeting or swim practice or soccer or scouts. I rush to get dishes done or I know I will be up until eleven doing them later. I read to the little children and the big ones have their own books to read, homework is done, the clothes laid out for tomorrow. Yes, the shoes are there, I see them. I tuck my children in with prayers. Lights off, except for the nightlight in Grace's room.

Later in the evening when they are asleep, I come up again to cover them. "These eyes of mine have seen the Savior; a light to enlighten the nations." I spend moments over them, each an icon of God. If I were Mary I could not love the infant Jesus more than I love these children. How is it, then, that I meditate on her love for her child and not on my love for my children?

Perhaps it is because my love is so tainted with my own sin and haste. Perhaps because I know that the call to be a disciple will and must transform my sight so that I see everyone as a child of God and that no less is expected of me than to see each person as an icon of God, just as my own children are icons—and yet I have just punished one of them and put him to bed in anger.

And other children of God today have been awful to me. How can I see an icon of God behind the tarnished silver casing of the burning letter, the cutting remark, the thoughtless gesture?

By the time I reach the wing chair where I pray the evening office, I am like a snarling dog guarding a last bone. The wing chair should be a refuge from the death of the spirit like the horns of the altar. If it were not for the wing chair itself, I would skip the office because I am so tired and cross. I go to my chair partly because the place itself calls me and partly out of sheer willpower. I know the place is as sacred as the time in which I have vowed to join my feeble words to those of the church in the world.

The children are asleep, Pat is out, the telephone is off the hook for this half-hour, interruptions superseded by the summons of the work of God in prayer. The soothing candlelight and the gray shawl sometimes, but not always, make entering the holy place easier. Here I am confronted with the day that is past and the sins I have committed in it, and here I must confront God and the life I bear within that must be born. At vespers I pray for those I love and for those I do not love and for those who do not love me, day after day. But the harshness of others is softened by prayer and candlelight and the displacement of time that occurs in the wing chair.

It is here, in the place and time set aside for prayer, that my soul magnifies the Lord like a lens meant to increase the clarity of divine love within all of us. Saying the same words night after night, like a child upstairs going to sleep, I am learning that as menial as my tasks are, and as sinful as I am, God has remembered his promise of mercy, in ordinary time.

sixteen

Crosswalk

O LORD, I have heard of your renown,
  and I stand in awe, O LORD, of your work.
In our own time revive it;
  in our own time make it known;
    in wrath may you remember mercy. (Habakkuk 3:2)

The telephone rang at the most hectic time of day.

"Please come get me?"

"Jack, you can walk home, it's only two blocks!"

"But Mom, I'm tired and my saxophone case is too heavy to carry all that way. Please come and get me in the car. Please?"

"Oh, Jack, okay, but I'm not happy about it."

I turned off the stove, put on shoes and lipstick, and gave motherly instructions to Trevor and Grace to be good. I dressed the baby and strapped him into the carseat. I drove along Waterman Boulevard, over the crosswalk, to his teacher's house, where Jack was waiting outside, managing to look both angelic and ingratiating.

A moment later I was again at the crosswalk. A red sports car was sprawled at an angle across the middle of the road with its warning lights flashing. Beyond that, a twisted bicycle and a tennis shoe. An unconscious boy was lying in the road. A man knelt over the boy, calling out to no one, "We're losing his pulse!"

"Has an ambulance been called?"

"Yes."

"Is there something I can do?"

"No. I was coming to wait for my daughter at the crosswalk. The driver said the kid came out of nowhere. Do you know this kid?"

The child looked exactly Jack's age.

I turned back to the car. "Jack, do you know the boy?"

"No, Mom, but I can't really look at him."

"Oh, Jack, pray as hard as you can!"

Jack bowed his head and folded his hands. But I prayed as adults pray, smashing my fists against the steering wheel and crying, pounding on the closed gates of heaven, begging for heaven to open, to intervene, to change the course of time, as if God were asleep and needed to be awakened by pleading and shouting.

By the time the police arrived, the baby was fussing in his carseat and Jack was begging me to take him home. I drove the children to the house and returned alone on foot. An ambulance arrived and by now there was a large crowd. A young man stood where I had been praying, also weeping, stamping his feet in anger and fear and horror as the medics painstakingly lifted the child off the pavement. A black and white hightop tennis shoe lying on its side was left on the street, its laces long and limp.

My afternoon continued with shocking normalcy. The children quarrelled, I cooked dinner, they tackled homework reluctantly. The table was set, dishes done, parish phone calls made, and then the children's bathtime and bedtime. Evening prayer was softened by the darkness and the familiar words. "Keep watch, dear Lord, with those who work or watch or weep this night...." Is the boy alive? Did the police find out his name? Do his parents know about the accident yet? I thought of our prayers in the car. Jack and I begging God to stop the horror, for the accident not to have happened, for God to save the boy's life, for everything to be all right.

Is it wrong to pray, like Joshua, for time to stop? Or to ask, like Habakkuk, for the revival of God's mighty deeds "in our own time"? I cannot merely be thankful that the tragedy did not happen to me. Prayer breaks down the illusion of separateness between the victim, the unwilling agent of evil, and those of us who believe we are watching from the outer circle of spectators.

As the boy had lain unconscious in the crosswalk, an older man had pushed through the crowd to put his arms around the teenaged driver. This man's loving response made me think of the spheres of love surrounding children: how would the child's parents relate to the teenaged boy? Or this young man's father to the victim's parents? Separated by minutes, we stand within entirely different spheres. In one sphere, a teenager rushing to pick up his tuxedo—the speed impressed his girlfriend, his friends told me—a girlfriend, and a father. In another, a little boy on his way to play, his father and mother who love him. In another, my son with his saxophone case, his father and siblings, myself as an observer. At times in prayer I find that these separate spheres overlap. I am in the boy's mother waiting in the hospital; she is in my praying at the steering wheel for heaven to turn back time. We are in both the carefree young man racing his car and the boy lying unconscious in the crosswalk.

Maybe I am praying because the boy's parents can't; in tragedy it is impossible to pray. Or perhaps I am praying out of my own fear of the time when I might be confronted with the ground crying with my children's blood, or blood that they have spilled. One day I will have to hand them the car keys.

The morning after the accident, a moment—the length of time of a red light—separated the young driver and me from meeting again. We were both on the same errand at the same time, to buy a newspaper at the gas station. I wanted to know if the child had been identified. Indeed, I wanted to know if he had survived the night.

The young man drove a different car. Leaning up against it at the gas station, he opened the paper to read. I waited for the light to change. I realized that if he stayed to continue reading, I would have to speak to him. Like yesterday, I watched him from the side of the road. Like yesterday, he did not notice me. What would I say to him? I was confronted with a confusion of compassion and dread. I suppose I would introduce myself and formally offer to be someone he could talk with if he had no one else. My inner feelings of failure were brought to light by the wait at the traffic signal. But he got into his car and left just as the light changed. Only such a moment of time had separated the fate of that boy from my own son.

This is what I pray: do not bring us to the test. Do not test my love beyond my capacity to love. Do not test my lovelessness. And deliver us from evil.

In the newspaper there is a picture of the sports car and the single shoe on the crosswalk. The boy's name is Bobby.

---

seventeen

Room for Another

I remember having a rather nervous lunch with my bishop a few years ago after I'd been a seminary student for over ten years, studying part-time during the pregnancy, birth, and raising of three children and our military transfers from Washington, D.C. to Texas to California.

During lunch I had to tell my bishop that after all those moves, the patchwork studies, the practicums, the clinical pastoral education, the completing of interviews and ordination exams, after making my way through all the long series of "hoops" that complete the requirements for ordination, after being hired by a church and finally getting my youngest child into school, I found that I was pregnant again. I was terrified that the purpose of our lunch—to look at ordination dates and celebrate the passing through of all those hoops—might be in vain. I had no idea what my bishop would say or what would happen to our plans as I told him about this unforeseen circumstance.

He smiled. "I wouldn't worry about it. I would think everyone would just move over a bit and make room for one more."

And it came to pass as my bishop said. Not only in our family but in the church as well, everyone moved over and made room for a little redhead named Patrick.

Making room for Patrick meant replacing a desk with a crib in the little catch-all room we used as a study and guest room. Patrick loves his room and talks his way through the religious pictures: an icon cross I bought at the Camaldolese monastery in Italy, a picture of Our Lady of Guadalupe from our San Antonio days, a marble copy of the face of Mary from Michelangelo's *Pietà* that our priest gave us for my ordination, a drawing of the Empty Tomb by a friend.

Patrick also talks about the giant cross at St. Martin's that hangs over the altar. He loves everything that has to do with the sphere of God, and when he goes to sleep at night we sing a song about how Jesus loves Patrick and Jesus wants Patrick to love him, too. Then we sing the song through the whole family: Daddy and Mommy and Trevor and Jack and Grace, how Jesus loves each of us and wants us to love him. And if Patrick's eyelids are not heavy by that time, we sometimes sing through the beloved toys in his bed: Raccoon, Bubby, Bear-Bear, Dragon, Darth Vader.

Patrick's song helps remind me of my own work of intercessory prayer, when I try to hold others in my heart and commend them to God. By taking others into my heart I dedicate myself to a wider sphere of life. In prayer, the wideness of my heart is open before God, and how much room my heart can hold depends upon how I live my life.

My heart can be crowded not only with my own concerns but with ulterior motives. Maybe I'm praying for someone because I think they ought to conform to my own idea of perfection. Sometimes "intercession" can be interchangeable with "interference," as in "her mother-in-law likes to intercede in family matters on her son's behalf." I have heard that some intercessory prayers do "intercept" in the sense of interfering, such as the cancer patient who tells her daughter to stop praying for her because the prayers are holding her back from a merciful and swift death.

Self-dedication to prayer requires humility and relinquishing of motives and the illusion of power or control. Prayer teaches me that my children, my friends, my church, my community, the whole world, belong to God. In intercessory prayer I acknowledge this truth over and over because the relinquishing of my world to God is against my nature.

But while intercessory prayer asks for a relinquishing of personal manipulation, it also presents the call to enter the mind of God and carry through the will of God in our actions. If I take on the responsibility of praying for human rights, I should not be surprised to find myself writing letters for Amnesty International or carefully monitoring the voting of my congressional representatives. If I pray for a friend with AIDS, I should not be surprised when a diocesan conference asks me to write a meditation for people suffering from the illness or to speak at a conference.

If prayer widens my heart to embrace spheres beyond myself, I should not be surprised to find myself walking in those spheres. If I pray daily for a neighborhood boy hit by a car, I should not be surprised to find myself calling the intensive care physician, who happens to be a friend, to follow the boy's progress. I should not be surprised to find myself invited to visit Bobby's bedside or to spend a few hours a week during his rehabilitation singing to him and telling knock-knock jokes.

Like every other form of prayer, intercession is a matter of a lifetime's learning and practice. Patrick's world extends hardly beyond his family and his toys. Daily, however, his world widens, gaining depth and breadth, and his prayer will have to widen, too.

Grace's prayer at bedtime describes the world she sees outside her window. We begin with the hills that frame the horizon, then the horse pasture and the neighbor's trees, coming closer and closer toward her window until we pray for Grace herself.

Goodnight hills, goodnight trees,
Goodnight windmills, goodnight breeze,
Goodnight fences, goodnight flowers,
Goodnight to the nighttime hours.
Goodnight deck, goodnight chair,
Goodnight insects everywhere.

Goodnight roof and goodnight sky,
   Goodnight nighttime birds that fly.
God bless Dad and God bless Mom,
   Please keep our family safe from harm.
God bless Patrick, Jack, and Trevor,
   Keep us in Your love forever.
God bless the world and God bless Grace
   May we all see You face to face. Amen.

We argue sometimes about adding petitions because her universe has expanded considerably since we composed the prayer in her childhood. I insist, however, that she keep the line "God bless the world and God bless Grace" intact because I want her to know that the biggest thing—the world—is as important as the littlest thing—Grace—and that Grace is as important as the world. Somehow, mysteriously, the world and Grace are bound up with each other.

I hope, too, that she hears "May we *all* see You face to face." Intercessory prayer anticipates the great reconciliation at the end of time when we stand together, with room for all, friend and enemy alike, unmasked before God in pure joy.

eighteen

A Habit of Gratitude

In a time of favor I have answered you,
   on a day of salvation I have helped you. (Isaiah 49:8)

I have a very well-worn white and turquoise Penguin paperback book whose cover is stained with water, tears, and the ring of a coffee cup. The corners have gradually frayed away, the spine is beginning to come apart, and the fragile pages have turned dark. The book smells like an old attic. The print now seems too small for my middle-aged eyes.

When I need to consult this book I handle a new copy in a different edition. I keep the old one wrapped in cellophane and take it out from time to time in a habit of gratitude, because this particular copy once saved my life.

At the age of twenty-two, just after graduating from college and a year into marriage, I found myself in what I now know was a clinical depression. In retrospect there are many reasons why this could have occurred, but at the time, knowing nothing of depression, I thought of it only as a matter of losing faith.

Faith is a real substance to me. When I wake in the morning, faith enables me to move my body to sit up in bed, put my feet on the floor, and walk to the bathroom or make coffee or feed the cat. Faith gives reasons to eat breakfast and dress and fix my hair; it knows that my actions are not random or meaningless. So at twenty-two, without meaning and without faith, I could not function. Time dragged so heavily that every movement of my body seemed to take a lifetime. To move my arms or legs, to lift a cup of water, to put on a blouse, made me feel, to the extent that I could feel anything, like Atlas holding up the world.

After my senior flute recital and graduation from college, my husband and I housesat for a couple who were traveling in Europe. While he studied at night for his first set of medical boards, I would sit on the concrete back steps drinking Greek wine and watching the highway, wondering how most efficiently to end my life.

Depression does not need a cause or a reason to consume a life. I know now that my depression had biological and emotional causes, but what I thought at the time was that God had abandoned me. The "life force," "creative daemon," "holy spirit"—those many ambiguous names for something far more real than myself—disappeared. Since birth this sense of another life seemed to come through the top of my head and propel me into a dance of reverence and wonder; now I felt like a body without a soul.

If hell is a state of being without God, I was experiencing it. I decided against ending my life on the highway, but careful, meticulous planning of another way to die occupied my time. Outwardly I remained cheerful and normal, as silently, night and day, I worked on my plans, knowing my release depended upon absolute precision and secrecy.

My husband and I traveled in England that summer, visiting friends. The day we left my friend Julian's house, he suggested we go to the Black Horse Bookstore near the train station in Norwich to buy "a read for the train." Depression makes it impossible to be interested in anything, and so I was surprised when I found my hand drawn to a book on a wire rack in the religion section, which was housed in the basement. I took the paperback to the counter and paid for it, and then we picked up our backpacks and went to the train.

I remember green fields and thicket hedges, grazing sheep, village houses with small front gardens crammed with flowers, and stone churches with square Norman towers passing by outside the window of the train. I took my new turquoise and white book and began to read.

I had no idea what I was getting into. Within a few minutes, the autobiography of Teresa of Avila transformed my life as I became immersed in the voice of a woman from Spain speaking to me across a span of four hundred years. Page headings such as "All fuss is a mistake," "Not only a woman but wicked," "Do not be distressed," "On not straining," and "Waiting for God" confused and fascinated me. She described experiences like a "state of prayer" in ways I understood to be very much like my "creative state." My own "inner voice" was confirmed by her vivid stories. I knew well her "very fleeting" experience of the profound "presence of God as made it impossible for me to doubt He was within me, or that I was engulfed in Him."

Teresa compared the stages of prayer to four ways of watering a garden "of unfruitful soil which abounds in weeds." You can draw up water from a well with a bucket, which takes a lot of effort, or a windlass can draw the water for you, which is a bit easier. Even better, a stream may flow through the garden. But for God to water the garden with lifegiving rain is the best way and certainly the most effortless.

I hadn't a clue as to what she was talking about; to me, prayer meant the Book of Common Prayer or the Lord's Prayer. But everything she talked about was connected to my own life—my playing jazz and writing poetry, the lifelong connectedness to and the recent disconnection from God. Teresa said, "I was much harmed at the time by not knowing that one can see things with other eyes than those of the body."

Her teaching on prayer implied a disciplined life of devotion and she offered liberal advice for "beginners," who must draw the water for the garden from the deep well with a heavy bucket. Beginners? What this meant, I couldn't know. But because of her utter candidness and humor and the sheer hubris of her struggle to describe the undescribable, I knew that her book was true in a way I had not experienced truth before. I realized that prayer—whatever it was—would become, even more than music, the central art of my life. And I vowed that when I returned to our apartment in Washington I would find someone to teach me to pray.

I don't read Teresa's autobiography much anymore. She led me to other teachers as time went on. But I remember her humor, her unrelenting honesty, her struggles in writing her experiences down, and the unseen hand that drew my hand to her book and saved my life.

I never want to experience the hell of a serious depression again, but in an odd way I am grateful. Those few months of unbearable pain may have saved me a lifetime of struggling to find my way or a lifetime of believing I was crazy. Teresa taught me that reverence, love of God, worship, and the sense of something far more real than myself beyond what the "bodily eyes" can see are simply a part of normal Christian living.

I often forget thanksgiving as a discipline of prayer, especially when my faith occasionally begins to unravel like the spine of my precious copy of St. Teresa's life. Then I unwrap my book and enjoy the soft whir of the pages fanning through my fingers, my mysterious underlinings and penciled margin notes, the scent of an old attic. She comes to me. My eyes sting a bit, and I am grateful.

nineteen
Pillar of Cloud

When it rains I feel the heaviness of the presence of God. *Behold, I cover the roof, I knock, I surround you with my love, my power, my presence, my gentle litany.* When I think of deep prayer it is this winter prayer, when the rain comes, the clouds darkening the valley like a hand over a cup and covering the mountains, rain beating steadily at the pavement, the plants, the dirt, and the roof just over me. I am absorbed in this prayer and I breathe God.

The huge fire fed with heavy oak logs blazes with the presence of God in my workroom, a theophany within a theophany. In my solitude I hear only the hiss of the steam iron, the click of the washing machine from the garage, the constant love-patter spilling from the gutter pipe. I am listening, drunk with love.

Last night the streets flooded. Pat and I went out in boots to watch the water rise above the sidewalks. The power of the underground stream had burst open two sewer tops, which Pat replaced with a crowbar. At the top of our street the artificial banks of the stream, meant to subdue the flow and send the water underground, had burst, washing several inches of muddy water through two houses.

Thirty people have died in this storm. Three children were buried alive when a mountain spilled into their bedroom and their parents, helpless and listening, squeezed through a window as tons of mud silenced their children's screams. Bridges are gone, towns washed away, two hundred people on the other side of Highway 80 wait in a Red Cross shelter they reached by dinghy.

And yet I am absorbed in God in the rain.

Today I wash and iron but I would hardly call what I am doing work. This paltry pile of ironing does not at all justify an afternoon's work. What have I been doing, really? Resting? Relaxing my brain? Procrastinating? Puttering around downstairs with the iron on, occasionally adding a log to the fire? Where did the time go?

These few hours were utterly wasted, unused, unproductive, without future or past, time spent without worrying, planning, or organizing. I have to be careful not to feel guilty. Like parents who cannot bear to see their children dream or pretend because such play does not teach them anything useful, our culture demands a measurable and material profit from time. Yet all major world religions subvert this aspect of time. Awe is prayer in the immediate moment, the heart lifted into the cloud of divine presence. Adoration, as frivolous as love, is contemplation with no regard for time, meaning, accomplishment, interpretation, or under-standing in that moment.

When they were in the cloud with Jesus on the Mount of Transfiguration, did the disciples know what they came to understand later, after Jesus' resurrection? Did they know at the time that the figures with Jesus really were Elijah and Moses? Was Elijah accompanied by a raven, a jar of oil, a bolt of lightning? Did Moses have horns and carry stone tab-lets? Did they know that they beheld the law and the proph-ets? Did it matter? Probably not.

In retrospect, James, John, and Peter knew that Jesus was transfigured, that he went directly to Jerusalem to face his crucifixion, and what they saw and heard revealed in the cloud on the mountain was part of the history of salvation.

Suddenly a bright cloud overshadowed them, and from the cloud a voice said, "This is my Son, the Beloved; with him I am well pleased; listen to him!" (Matthew 17:5)

What understanding could there have been for the disciples at the time of their sleepy ecstasy? It was enough simply to be present to the divine presence.

Adoration is an aspect of prayer that has no need to un-derstand, plead, or clarify. It suspends time in the luminous moment of presence. Within this cloud enveloping the house, the silence, the solitude, the smell of woodsmoke, I somehow know this prayer of adoration, and for now, although I can-not understand, I accept awe as a gift. Awe is not always illu-minating or beautiful. Just as rain often lifts my heart toward contemplation, it also evokes fear—fear of fierce thunderstorms, of floods, of mudslides here in California.

In my workroom by the fire with the efficient steam iron and the boiling tea kettle I ask, is the rain God? Is God in the rain? Or did God die with the children in the mudslide, leaving the father and mother grieving, devastated, broken like their house under the mountain, their hearts buried in tons of mud?

The rain is not God and God is not in the rain. Because rain gives life, because of my love of life, because of my love of solitude, and because I can be found by God in my solitude, the rain makes a mirror of my soul and I see my soul reflected in the rain. I see what is beyond the rain and not contained by it, but what I would not see without the rain.

The rain is real. The cold numbs my fingers. The sound of rain and burning logs penetrates the quiet. There are goosebumps over my body; the hot coffee warms my hands. I watch the soft, transparent vapor rising from the cup. Steam warms, then wets my nose, the smell of fresh grounds released by the boiling water permeates the room. I drink.

God is real. God is more real than the rain. Or coffee. Or vapor. Or heat or cold. I breathe God. And when I do not cling with all my senses to the rain, the cold, the coffee, God's Reality invades, and leaves everything empty.

MY MOTHER'S STUDIO

Lent ◆ Season of Insight

twenty

Hospital Corridor

Remember that you are dust, and to dust you shall return.
(Liturgy of Ash Wednesday)

No light, but a red glow fills the sky in the east far away beyond the flightline as I drive toward the military base hospital. The giant cargo engines wail lamentations from one
horizon to another at a deafening pitch. When I get out of
the car the wind stings my ears. I put a quarter in a machine
near the hospital door and take a newspaper as a hold on
the world, as an amusement, an escape.

I wait in line. My blood is drawn into tubes with colored
stoppers. I drink a bottle of glucose and fight nausea for two
hours, trying to lose myself in the newspaper. Then my
blood will be drawn again and I can go out into the daylight,
go to church and be among friends, receive ashes upon my
head and impose ashes upon my friends in order to remind
one another we are but dust. The sanctuary is a place of love
and comfort. This hospital hallway with the fluorescent
lights overhead is drafty and impersonal; here, I do not
need to be reminded that I am but dust.

The sounds and smells of the hospital corridor almost always evoke the deep and timeless prayer of vigils spent by
the bedsides of my children. The smell of disinfectant and
betadine, the too-bright lights, the loud conversations in
hallways bring me to the edge of prayer, where the separa-
tion between life and death seems arbitrary and love overwhelming.

I feel again my face against the cool of the green wall of
the operating room surrounded by empty gurneys. Behind
the swinging doors doctors cut open my daughter's throat
and put in a tube so that she can breathe. I know by heart

the feel of the sticky vinyl chair, the sound of shouts, the beeps and clicks of heart monitor machines in the Intensive Care Unit where, for a week of nights and days, her frail little body fights off disease with risky, too-vigorous medicines. Jesus, she says, watches her from the folds of the plastic curtain.

I am by Trevor's bedside when he is not yet two years old, stroking his head, lulling him to an exhausted sleep only for him to scream himself awake in pain when his muscles contract in spasm around his broken leg each time he relaxes.

I relive the vigil from a rocking chair in a hidden corner of the hospital that my infant son Jack and I share with a monstrously deformed vegetable child. My newborn baby has fallen out of a basket and I do not know if he will recover his alertness. I lift again my son's grossly swollen head to nurse him at my breast. His dull eyes do not meet mine. I am utterly alone except for the older child in his cage-like bed, watching us.

I am holding a sixteen-month-old Jack down upon the debriding table in the burn ward, singing to him while the doctors painstakingly pull off the skin on his hands and feet twice a day. He was badly burned by an overheated Texas floor furnace and to this day Jack's scars shock any uninitiated priest giving communion into his outstretched hands. After eleven years his voice is still hoarse from nodules on his larynx caused by weeks of screaming in pain. He will still have to have an operation on his feet.

I guarded over my children's suffering through these nights and days. Maternal love could do nothing to take the pain away, and so I sang their names over and over and over.

Trevor and Jack and Grace did survive those traumas and I thankfully attributed their healing to God. But my neighbor's child of Grace's age did not survive a similar illness, and when Jack and I left the corner room with his head its normal shape again, we left the monstrous child behind, still tied to his crib. I know that the prayers of those other parents and children were not less worthy than mine. I am not ungrateful, but I can't forget the children who were left behind and I do not know what my prayer or my love or my ministry would be like had I not carried my children out of the hospital corridors alive and whole. Yet I sensed at the time that God was present in death as well as in life. It was not a sense of comfort or assurance that I experienced, but a love that did not depend on life or death.

A hospital corridor can be a mysterious place, a terrible and holy threshold upon the boundary of the soul. Here you will find an opening through which you might apprehend and embrace unexperienced aspects of God. Uprooted from your ordinary days, the hospital confounds the peaceful soul with the realization that the God of daily living is also the God of sudden dying. The God of the comforting parish sanctuary is also the God of the Intensive Care Unit. The God of beeswax candle and incense is the God of vomit and pus; the God of white linen and embroidered chasuble is the God of plastic curtain and sweaty sheet; the God of organ and flute is the God of squeaky gurney wheels and crying children; the God of deep port wine and delicately embossed communion bread is the God of infected blood and wounded flesh.

The God of all those corridor smells and sights and sounds is also the God of profound silence. When despair has obliterated ordinary prayer, when the psalms fail and all words are stupid and meaningless, the mantle of loneliness surrounding me becomes a mantle of dark and wordless love. This darkness reveals the paradox of prayer: in the absence of God, all there is, is God.

twenty-one
Sign of the Covenant

I cannot get used to the riot of life here in early Lent. Unusual California trees gush fountains of blossoms as if time were speeded up. Clouds, too, appear as if in a time-lapsed film, rushing across the sky. Rhapsodic shifts of dark and sudden light run over the hills and bursts of rain fall on the green hills full of lupine even while the sun shines. Rainbows arc from hill to hill all the way to the horizon in morning and late afternoon. Neighbors wage continual warfare with electric shears against overgrown shrubs running wild. The transition from winter to summer is like a delirious Mardi Gras of color and life.

It has taken seven years of living in California for me to anticipate this transition. You can't really call it "spring" because it is not so much a season as it is a rush toward summer. Neighbors plant in the fall or during the rains, and by Lent everything is blooming. By the time it occurs to me to plant vegetables, my neighbor's zucchini vines choke the garden.

This year, for the first time, flowers I planted in front of the house bloom in profusion. This success is due not just to timing, but to my giving up clinging to childhood favorites that love the cooler eastern weather. Last year I studied the plants that survive at the hot windy miniature golf course on the highway in Fairfield and planted accordingly: a hearty variety of snapdragon, calendulas, shasta daisy, candytuft, and a definitely non-English, non-French, non-aromatic lavender of some heathen variety. Why did it take me seven years to resist the stubborn temptation to plant an English herbaceous border?

I have a friend who fights the California environment with a successful "cottage garden" that she seems to work on almost full-time with manual help from her husband. She has a fresh, homegrown source of turkey, chicken, and rabbit droppings to keep the soil fertile and pliant, enhanced with commercial plant food and much water dripped in constantly, and the garden is fenced in and protected under the shade of huge trees. She is a garden lover and has an experienced hand. The results delight me, and I love to sit and watch her garden.

My front yard patch is all I can manage.

My friend suggested that I plant renunculas. The bulbs are twisted ugly little spidery dry things. I was not sure which way they went into the ground, so planting them right-side up was a matter of chance, or maybe faith, and despite bicycles, football games, and hide and seek, they have survived. Green shoots rose like a fleur-de-lis and then yielded elaborate leafy flourishes with protruding tight-fisted buds, like poppies. Renunculas bloom suddenly into bursts of crepe paper flowers with many petals crushed together and packed tightly in the middle by a solid stamen.

My front yard is lovely, but these pentecostal colors are disconcerting in Lent. Somehow I am not in touch with the seasons as they are in California; I still think of Lent as cold, windy, rainy, with only the slowest, barest hints of the coming life. Furthermore, the riot of life in even my front yard does not reflect the season of my soul. I cannot feel the beautiful colors, my spirit does not sway with the blossoms in the wind. The flowers do not lift my heart to God and I am ashamed that I am tempted to despair.

A teacher in seminary told me, "Pray as you can, not as you can't." I look at the vivid renuncula blossoms and feel nothing, but I remember the spidery dry bulbs with recognition. My soul is like those bulbs, dry and unpromising. Faith is like my friend's suggestion to plant the bulbs. I watch the plants grow and bloom and I know the soul is not dry always. I have lived this cycle of growing and dying and death and birth before.

> God said, "This is the sign of the covenant that I make between me and you and every living creature that is with you, for all future generations: I have set my bow in the clouds, and it shall be a sign of the covenant between me and the earth." (Genesis 9:12-13)

Life flourishes all about me, the skies sing and rainbows appear and disappear, the pentecostal colors of my flowers draw all eyes to the front yard patch. I go about my work, pray with people who ask me to, say the daily offices, preside at the eucharist. Family life proceeds in its normal, noisy, and happy chaos. Can people tell that I am saying the words but not praying them?

"Pray as you can, not as you can't." What if I can't pray at all? Then, I pray the non-prayer of dryness, the darkness of my soul, hidden in silence like the bulb underground, faithful to the sense of loss. If I feel loss, there must have been something to lose in the first place.

twenty-two

Bulldozers

One afternoon when I was about twelve years old I hurried into my mother's room after school, where I usually found her reading at that time of day.

"What is that noise outside?" I asked.

"Bulldozers," she replied.

"What for? What are they doing?"

"Housing development."

I ran outside. Bulldozers roared in a field adjacent to the woods behind our house. I saw the yellow metal machines crushing a row of delicate locust trees, the tangle of sumac bushes we called the jungle maze, the long grass, the elephant ear, the rare goat's rue, the tall stalks of mullein. I can think of nothing closer to the death of my own body than this apocalypse, the destruction of the holy places of my childhood.

Our days are like the grass;
   we flourish like a flower of the field;
When the wind goes over it, it is gone,
   and its place shall know it no more (Psalm 103:15-16)

Georgie, my next door neighbor, loved the woods as I did. Together we discovered places that other kids never knew because he, too, had a reverence for the oak woods. Georgie never let on to other children where the best wild strawberries grew, nor the sweetest blueberries. He protected the animals' holes, nests, and thickets and he had a secret source of arrowheads. Once we spent an afternoon counting Lady's Slippers, one hundred and twenty-seven of them, including an albino. It never occurred to us to pick them.

The day the bulldozers came, Georgie and I entered a silent pact and waged a holy war. When it was quiet at dusk and the workmen had left, we pulled out all the builder's marking stakes and hid them. We sabotaged the building site often, but if the builders ever noticed we never knew about it; the destruction proceeded relentlessly as bulldozers uprooted trees, pushing them into piles to be burned. For two years the fires rose day by day all around us. The bulldozers easily tore up the residue of centuries of oak leaves, a delicate black crust of loam over sand. The bulldozers turned up sand, sand on sand, and in less than an hour had destroyed what thin and fragile life had existed there.

Holy place by holy place was destroyed—the golden beeches on the slope, the twin hills full of blueberries in summer and asters in the fall, the only place we had a view in winter and the first place to reveal its buds in spring. There were no hills after the bulldozers; these hills, after all, were only large sandpiles left by the retreating glacier millions of years ago and were easily leveled. The stream bed, the arbutus, the ancient orchard, and the pond that filled with white apple blossoms in spring—all vanished into the sand.

Once the fields and woods had become sand, the land became a desert of houses all looking alike: plastic swimming pools and barking dogs, chain link fences and stiff new bushes from the nursery, stripling trees like twigs held up by thick stakes. The pond exerted its revenge by perpetually flooding a basement, but it was a scant victory.

My religion came from the woods and from the oak trees. Could God exist without the trees in which to live and breathe? Could I ever know God without the oak trees whispering God? Where would the red fox go? The almost tame herd of deer? Where would the hawk rest? If the woods, which God had made and where God dwelled and where God was manifest, could be stripped and burned, was the world and life itself destined for annihilation?

Armageddon had come to the woods but I was still alive. My universe, reconfigured, allowed for the death of God—unless God, though immanent in oak trees, was not confined to oak trees. My vision became less material. The limitless landscape of my childhood turned inward and became the landscape of my soul. Without oak trees as prayer, I prayed with my heart. Paradise, removed from me, was born again within me.

Birth is traumatic, so traumatic there is no memory of it. Perhaps the trauma of birth is better forgotten than remembered. Remembering would paralyze life. Fear of death may simply be the residual memory of birth. Or, perhaps, it is the opposite: perhaps human beings fear death because we have forgotten what it is like to be born into life.

I still hate the houses that stand in the place of the woods, even these thirty years later. How often I have wished for the woods, the smell of arbutus, the cascades of apple blossoms falling like snow, the taste of strawberries warmed by sun and sweet blueberries eaten by the mouthful, lying down on the hill. I still miss the accessibility of Paradise, the Garden of Eden, the womb of my soul.

But God did not leave me when my universe was overturned and burned. If anything, God became more intimate. I learned to pray, just as once I learned to breathe.

twenty-three

My Mother's Studio

Your sun shall no more go down,
or your moon withdraw itself;
for the LORD will be your everlasting light,
and your days of mourning shall be ended (Isaiah 60:20)

Shortly after I was married my mother confided that her ophthalmologist had told her that her eyes could "go at any time." The blindness that had been inherited for generations in our family would soon claim her. The vision in that one eye that saw so much was now dependent upon one strand of viable retina. She had been operated on so many times the latticework had completely degenerated.

Not long after she spoke to me, a call came from my father to say that my mother was in the hospital because she had lost her sight. I took a plane from Washington, D.C., where Pat and I lived, to stay with my family on Long Island. From there I could visit the hospital in New York City where my mother was being evaluated.

When I arrived home at midday and went into the house, it was dark inside. My father had drawn all the drapes. He who had always gotten sick when my mother was away could not be persuaded to let light into the house. After putting away my things, I went up to my old room with the views to the north and south and the large eastern window, the room my mother used as her studio. Even here it was dark and the curtains were drawn. On a table near her easel my mother had arranged an odd assortment of dark objects on a black velvet cloth. She had been painting a somber still life and her pallet was laid aside as if she'd just put it down, mixed with interesting splotches of oil paint—all shades of black.

Perhaps my mother's extraordinary vision was a kind of hoarding, based upon the principle that her sight was always threatened and therefore precious. She lived as if garnering everything she saw, amassing a wealth of visual impressions through painting, drawing, making things, gazing through the telescope, peering at minute things with her one myopic eye, her glasses askew on her forehead. I once asked her if she thought the threat of blindness taught her to see. She thought about it carefully, then replied she did not know.

I can't speak for my mother because her story is different from my own, but I associate her ability to see with my willingness to pray. I think I pray because she saw so much. I do not see things the way my mother did and I take eyesight for granted, but I did learn the fundamental principle behind the way she looked at things: continually discovering the extraordinary behind the ordinary. She said as much to us when we would misplace something and she'd scold, "Look behind! Look under! Look over! Look around!"

When I am not seeing as she taught me to see, I feel as though I am in sin. If I am too busy to see, to feel, to be aware of the numinous blazing behind the starfish, the shell, the petrified wood, I am not living. I am wasting my life. I am most intensely alive when I pray. Prayer is to me what painting was to my mother: a way of seeing and of knowing, a way of loving life. Not to pray is deliberately to stop seeing, to stop knowing, to withdraw from living.

My mother did not have peripheral vision. She was awkward, always bumping into things. The darkness on the periphery threatened to obscure the light, but it also intensified what she was able to see. I learned from her sightedness and from her blindness that what happens within the short span of life is infinitely precious.

I would be more myself and more alive if I could remember to love life with the passion I had as a child. In winter I *had* to scrape bits of frost off the east window with my fingernail and taste it, and watch the sunrise turn the silver window to gold and pink until the crystals finally broke apart into many lesser worlds and melted, because tomorrow was a hundred years away and I might never see frost again. On summer evenings I knelt at the window watching the shades of green change with the breeze across the tops of the oak trees as far as I could see, delighting in the scent from the woods coming into my room, letting my soul ride upon the gracefulness of the swallow circling between the houses on a damp evening.

For many years after she lost her sight, my mother held on to the hope that she would be able to see again. In the first few years she would even occasionally think she caught a glimpse of something—the refrigerator door or a banana—and wish she could have seen something more interesting, like her first grandchild. Naturally we tried to make up for her not being able to see by describing what things looked like. My mother's father, who was also blind, could listen endlessly to our descriptions but my mother would say crossly, "Stop describing things to me! I get my impressions other ways."

She hated acquaintances she called "Job's comforters," people who said, "Be glad you could see for as long as you could!" or "Be glad that you can still hear!" Her response was caustic but typically honest: "I am *not* glad." Blindness was as close to dying as she could get.

When I went into New York to visit my mother in the hospital, her room was brightly lit and high up in the building, with a view of the city. Her roommate was charming and funny, and we had a good time. I stayed long enough to read the Sunday comics and other parts of the newspaper aloud to her in the cheerful room. That afternoon I took the train back to Washington, to my husband, to college, to my own new life, leaving something irrevocably behind, not having said anything, not having understood.

twenty-four
Refusing to Pray

There are times, long times, sometimes months, when I refuse to pray. I avoid the wing chair, never light a candle, never move the ribbons in my prayer book because if I read the words I might be moved to pray—or worse, might not be moved to pray.

Sometimes I refuse to pray when life crowds me. The relentless demands of family and church, the crises at home and at work, the noise and busyness, all play their part in the chaos of modern life where there is so much to do I do only what has to be done immediately. It seems to me that after a time all the things that make life beautiful and worthwhile, like the quiet and slow building of projects or relationships, the gradual exercise of conscious virtue, the setting apart of time for the practice of reflection, even prayer, become expendable. I live life at a pace where daily living becomes a series of interruptions interrupting interruptions, like throwing snapshots into a box before you look at them and finally giving up trying to take pictures at all.

My willful retreat from prayer makes me think of the Israelites in the desert at Massah and Meribah. The Israelites had already experienced the Passover, the escape from Egypt, the parting of the Red Sea, the continual presence of God in the pillar of cloud and fire guiding them. They had already beheld a miracle: after three days without water in the wilderness of Shur, Moses threw a log into the spring, turning the bitter water sweet. They camped at an oasis with twelve springs and seventy palm trees. Daily they ate manna, and once, when they were hungry for meat, feasted on a miraculous flock of quails.

But when again there was no water, they blamed Moses:

> *The people thirsted there for water; and the people complained against Moses and said, "Why did you bring us out of Egypt, to kill us and our children and livestock with thirst?" (Exodus 17:3)*

The Lord told Moses to take the rod with which he had touched the Nile and strike a rock on Mount Horeb. Moses did, and water came out of the rock for the people to drink.

He called the place Massah and Meribah, because the Isra-
elites quarreled and tested the LORD, saying, "Is the LORD
among us or not?" (Exodus 17:7)

After so many extraordinary miracles, why didn't the Israelites have the faith to believe they would be provided for?
And why do I ask, "Is the Lord among us or not?"

From the beginning I sensed that I was made for reverence. My first memory is of sitting on my kiddie-car in our
backyard near the white picket fence, with blue sky, clouds,
an airplane, the scent of apple blossoms above me. I had no
words for blossoms, airplane, or sky, but I remember that
moment of stunning awareness I now recognize as "religious." I was created for worship.

Throughout my life I have never doubted that I was led
out of Egypt through stages of the wilderness. I try to remember that I have been loved, drawn and guided in secret
and in the open, sustained by the Holy One in the dark and
in the light. But my memory is about as good as that of the
Israelites, especially if I have not been praying. Thankfully,
my tradition draws me to God by other routes. When my
mind shuts out God, or the busyness of my life (or whatever
excuse I find to rebel against God this time) keeps me from
faithfulness, the ritual of the eucharist will hold me to faith.

Sometimes simply the beauty of the ritual itself will hold
my attention; sometimes it is a musical harmony or a turn of
phrase in the third verse of the hymn, or the church's sense
of spaciousness. Sometimes the scent of incense, candles,
and starched linen is all that I can appreciate, but its beauty
works on my senses while the underlying pattern of death
and resurrection renews itself in me. The prayers work inside of me even if I don't pray them, my heart takes in the
Word of God even if I don't listen, and the motions of the
liturgy guide me whether I practice the movements with fer-
vor or not.

One of my seminary professors came to chapel one day and just sat near the back, not speaking the words, never standing or singing. A group of first-year students approached him after chapel: "Why did you just sit there? Why didn't you participate in the liturgy?"

"Sometimes it is enough just to be there," he replied.

The liturgy itself and the community at prayer will carry me through this time. I can enter the space and time of worship and nothing is diminished because I can't pray. When my mind is too busy or too blank, when my faith is too fragile, when my own willfulness pits me against myself and the Holy, the community carries the memory and enacts the ritual. And then, of course, there are times when others can't pray and I can.

I wonder if it is possible that I can pray sometimes *because* at other times I refuse. If the Israelites had not argued with Moses, would they have been fit to go directly to Canaan? Would they have understood the cost? Would they have been able to pass along the strength and endurance, the fire and passion it would take the subsequent generations to become a holy people living in community with the law?

The Bible says that the Israelites traveled through the wilderness "by stages." Maybe these stages depended upon overcoming the various layers of their own natural rebelliousness, not to learn mindless submission, but to learn the value of memory. Without dispute and challenge, there is no need for memory. The Israelites would have been led like their flocks and herds through the desert without incident or conflict, without a story, without memory or the need for ritual.

I know, finally, that when I have gone away from faith and refused to pray long enough, it is time for me to recover the memory of the sacred events of my own life. And so I begin at the beginning and marvel once again at what God has done in my life. The ritual of telling my life to myself—beginning with the kiddie-car, the airplane, the fence, the times when the Lord was with me—is the beginning of prayer again.

twenty-five

The Rugged Terrain of My Heart

I am late. I lock the car and hurry across the parking lot, up a few steps, and push open a heavy oak door just enough to let me slip through. I enter the cool, dim church, the sound of traffic muted within the thick stone. High over me in a circle around the church, I acknowledge with a smile the presence of old friends I have prayed with, friendly saints surrounding me in blue stained glass. As my eyes adjust to the darkness, I notice the priest already in the church, waiting for me.

"Sorry. I got stuck."

"You're not late," says the priest. I know he is trying to tell me it is all right to be late, like the laborers hired at the end of the day who are still paid a full day's wages. We kneel at the altar rail with our prayer books.

Have mercy on me, O God,
    according to your loving-kindness;
        in your great compassion blot out my offenses.
Wash me through and through from my wickedness,
    and cleanse me from my sin.
For I know my transgressions only too well,
    and my sin is ever before me.

Holy God, Holy and Mighty, Holy Immortal One,
have mercy upon us.

I say, "Pray for me, a sinner," and the priest replies, "May God in his love enlighten your heart, that you may remember in truth all your sins and his unfailing mercy. Amen." He speaks the comforting words from Matthew, "Come unto me, all ye that travail and are heavy laden, and I will refresh you."

Now, in the presence of Christ, and of me, his minister, confess your sins with a humble and obedient heart....

Silence pervades the church. Our whispers seem safe and yet they are not absorbed by the vast space. Beams of morning light form pools upon the stone floor and the Oriental rug in the nave. This holy space comforts me; I remember leaving marks under my sweaty forearms where I leaned against the communion rail in prayer one summer's day. I remember wiping tears from the wood, and once I unbound my braid and wiped the foot of the altar with my hair and tears. I have danced alone here in the aisle in prayer. I often converse aloud with the lighted saints. I remember laughing in my prayer.

Holy God, heavenly Father, you formed me from the dust in your image and likeness, and redeemed me from sin and death by the cross of your Son Jesus Christ. Through the water of baptism you clothed me with the shining garment of his righteousness, and established me among your children in the kingdom. But I have squandered the inheritance of your saints, and have wandered far in a land that is waste. Especially, I confess to you and to the Church....

And I make my confession.

Silence again. The priest sighs. He asks me a couple of questions. Then he says, "Let's not go on. Let's talk for a while. Let's go outside." Absolution with this priest is never a foregone conclusion, at least not immediately. Being only sorry is not good enough. We take cushions from the prie-dieu at the back of the church and go to the garden to sit.

A church's garden represents paradise. Modern suburban churches find it hard to maintain a garden because, like the rest of life, church has become an activity on the run between appointments and obligations rather than a place to live. But an old church like this one, with a tradition reflecting another time, tries to preserve symbolisms lost to this generation. Its door is the gate of the heavenly Jerusalem, its baptismal font the water of life flowing through Paradise. The church courtyard is a place to meditate or walk or sit and remember, or look toward Paradise after all the sorrow and crying on earth is done. So we sit in Paradise, on stone benches with our cushions in the sun, surrounded by flowers, the scent of ancient boxwood warmed by heat.

I am talking to a very great sinner. I could not confess my sins to someone who did not understand the depths and agonies of sin and the acute frailty of human nature. How could I talk with someone who did not have compassion or empathy, who could not understand the importance of repentance, who could not agonize over his own sins or who did not have a passion for God? Knowing he is a sinner is a great comfort to me. And yet I know he is also Abraham, bargaining for mercy for his people; Moses, arguing with Yahweh; the shepherd leaving the other sheep in order to rescue me from the cliffs and crevices where I have become lost. This priest can find me because he knows these rocks and caverns in the rugged terrain of the human heart.

I am not surprised by the depth or extent of my own sins because I discovered the horror of evil dwelling in my heart at the age of four, during a summer visit to a farm belonging to cousins. At dusk, while the adults were in the lighted house talking, I was outside in the yard playing with a family of kittens. One of the kittens scratched me severely. Angrily, before I could think, I ran over to the well with it and threw it in. I realized instantly and horribly what I had done, but fortunately a heavy metal seal I had not seen in the dark covered the well and the kitten was unharmed.

I thought for a long time that night about what I had almost done. Since then I have realized in increasing increments how much worse it is not to know the human soul's capacity for evil than it is to face the horror of your heart. Evil most often occurs when you think you are doing good or when you trust yourself to be well-intentioned and therefore immune from wrong.

The priest and I talk for an hour about sin, willfulness, sloth, the way I live my life, the things that distract me from the Holy. Satisfied for the time being but with a promise that we will talk again and that I will be accountable to him for a while in certain things, we go back into the church.

Will you turn again to Christ as your Lord?
I will.

He places his hand upon my head as he gives me the words of absolution.

Now there is rejoicing in heaven; for you were lost, and are found; you were dead, and are now alive in Christ Jesus our Lord.

He adds, "Go in peace and pray for me, a sinner."

twenty-six

Night Watch

The baby cries in the night. I get up out of bed and go to the little room next to ours. I cover him with his blanket, comfort him, stroke his back gently until he falls back to sleep. The house is silent.

Fully awake now, I find my way to the wing chair in the living room. Darkness widens the boundaries of the room. The outline of the couches, bookcase, and piano fade into a darkness without walls. Squares of orange light from the street lamp, mixed with the patterns in the lace curtain, define the space of the room.

I had been in a beautiful dream when the baby woke me. I dreamed I was pregnant, which in itself might not be surprising since I have been pregnant a good part of my adult life. Now I no longer have a womb and I will not be pregnant again. The dream was not a foreshadowing and certainly not wishful thinking, but it so happens that this year I have often dreamed I am pregnant.

Sometimes my dream is frightening: I am alone or I am going to die in childbirth. At other times the pregnancy is secret and I have to hide it, or no one else can see it or understand or believe me. Sometimes the conscious self intrudes enough to cry out, "How can this be, since I have no womb?"

When Patrick, my last child, was born I was given a spinal anesthetic that allowed me to be awake for the operation. He was the only child of the four caesarian deliveries I was able to observe being born, and I revelled in his first wonderful cries. After the baby was safely born, had been admired for his red hair and perfect shape, his beauty and strength, the surgeon removed the well-worn womb from my body. He remembered our agreement and said to the nurse, "Suzanne wants to see her uterus."

She immediately obliged and held my uterus with long steel tongs, cervix end up, over a bucket near the operating table so that I could get a good look.

Friends have asked since, "Why ever in the world would you want to see your uterus?" Partly out of curiosity—I simply wondered what it looked like, just as, when a child, I wanted to see my first lost tooth. But my inverted uterus had also held a tyranny of pain over me for most of my life, each pregnancy and childbirth rendering the already misshapen thing more frail, uncomfortable, and perilous. After my second child, Jack, was born, I had been advised not to have more children. Pregnancy terrified me; another birth could mean my own death. Maybe by seeing my womb I just wanted to know for certain I would not have to face pregnancy again.

Even so, I perceived a sacred dimension to this womb that carried my children before birth, like any holy icon or relic that I wanted to see for all its fascinating ugliness. Perhaps I saw in it a symbol of the sacred in the mundane: our bodies bearing our souls for the duration of our pilgrimage on earth, glad for their past use but gladder still for their future uselessness, finally wearing out and letting us go.

So the sack that hid and nurtured that deep love in motherhood went to the incinerator, ashes ahead of the rest of my body.

Tonight my dream was not terrifying but beautiful, though I don't remember if there was a story to the dream or whether it was simply a wonderful image, like my memory of it. I was "great with child" and a voice whispered a phrase softly, several times. In different layers from dream consciousness into waking consciousness I heard it, insistent, so that I would not miss it: *"imago Dei,"* the image of God.

What can this mean? I am about to give birth, but then, am I also the one being born? Is the *imago Dei* being born within me? Am I carrying within me the image of God, ready to give birth in the fullness of time? This time, do I have anything to fear?

> *Do not remember the former things,*
> *or consider the things of old.*
> *I am about to do a new thing;*
> *now it springs forth, do you not perceive it?*
> *I will make a way in the wilderness*
> *and rivers in the desert. (Isaiah 43:18-19)*

Contemplative prayer is that way in the wilderness; the wandering itself becomes a way. Isaiah's promise of a way in the wilderness is a river in the desert, breaking through the wilderness of prayer.

Awakened by the cry of my son, attentive to the child and to the dream, I wait in this darkened room with pale orange light. Curled up in the wing chair, where in daylight I recite the prayer book office but cannot render words into prayer, tonight I wait in wonder and silence. Like a creature forming slowly in a womb close to Another's heart, I perceive a presence I cannot see because the presence is so near.

twenty-seven

Grace, My Zen Master

The congregation crowds into the parish hall for the liturgy of the palms. At the last minute we can't seem to get ourselves organized. Their voices become louder and louder as time goes on, impatient, almost raucous, the atmosphere of a party beginning to get out of hand. The acolytes squeal in panic: "We don't know what we're *do-ing!*"

"That's okay, none of us knows what we're doing," I reply. "Stay calm and try to look like you know what you're doing."

The young man carrying the cross and getting ready to lead the procession pipes up. "This happens every year! Every year we don't know what we're doing in Holy Week!"

"Not to know is part of holy tradition," I laugh, trying to put the acolytes at ease. "Why should you know more than the rest of us anyway?" I'm thinking to myself, "Next year come to the acolyte training meetings!" but I say aloud, "Just make sure the kids follow you to church school and I'll make sure the adults stay in the church, okay?"

Finally the crowd quiets down when someone places an armload of palms on a table in the center of the hall. The palms are blessed and distributed. The collect is read.

> *Assist us mercifully with your help, O Lord God of our salvation, that we may enter with joy upon the contemplation of those mighty acts, whereby you have given us life and immortality; through Jesus Christ our Lord. Amen.*

We listen to the gospel story of Jesus' triumphal entry from the Mount of Olives into Jerusalem:

> *A very large crowd spread their cloaks on the road, and others cut branches from the trees and spread them on the road. The crowds that went ahead of him and that followed were shouting, "Hosanna to the Son of David! Blessed is the one who comes in the name of the Lord! Hosanna in the highest heaven!" (Matthew 21:8-9)*

Acolytes, church school children, congregation, and priests march out of the parish hall into the parking lot, crying "Blessed is he who comes in the name of the Lord! Hosanna in the highest!" As I walk the wind whips at the blood-red chasuble, taunting, tormenting. I don't shout or sing as enthusiastically as I might.

My daughter Grace is not with the children. On the way to church she had said, "I don't want to be in the parade. But can I still get a palm?"

"All right," I had told her, "stay with your little brother in the nursery, but make sure you come to church for communion. I'll see that you get a palm later."

The rest of the church school follows the cross and the acolytes. What are the children thinking right now? Are they wondering why the donkey did not show up this year? Do they associate this walk through the parking lot with the triumphal entry of Jesus into Jerusalem? Are they thinking to themselves, "Today Jesus is King. He is Lord. It is finally fair. He is finally recognized for what he is"? I realize that my wondering about what the children are thinking is really a way to avoid what I am thinking: "Why are we doing this?"

We hear the organ playing, but the sound, seized by the wind, is erratic.

All glory, laud, and honor to thee, Redeemer, King!
to whom the lips of children made sweet hosannas ring.

We sing to the wind, but the wind snatches the song from our throats. The children process into the church, around the altar, and out the back door to go to church school. The rest of us remain. The same crowd that proclaimed him king in the parking lot will shout to crucify him while we are in the sanctuary.

I am playing Jesus this year in the reading of the Passion story, and I will not have to call for Barabbas or condemn Jesus. My eyes sting nevertheless. Whether I am Jesus for the gospel reading or not, I still have every opportunity to betray him.

As we stand for the reading about Golgotha, a small movement in the front row attracts my eye. Grace has slipped quietly into the church.

Now she knows. She can see us right here, betraying him. Maybe this is why she did not want to be in the "parade." Maybe she knew all along.

Jesus breathes his last. The Passion story is finished. As we sit down for the sermon, Grace makes her way to the chairs with the acolytes and priests where I am. The priest next to me approaches the pulpit and she takes his seat. First she leans against my shoulder, then she wiggles closer, just short of getting on my lap. She wraps my cincture around her waist.

The preacher, who is a philosopher, speaks about the history of the Christian doctrine of the atonement. I am glad this is an academic sermon because I don't want to have any feelings about the sacrifice of Christ in atonement for our sins right now. But I can't concentrate anyway.

Grace's shoe comes off with a barely audible *clok! clok!* Shoe off. Scrape. Shoe on. *Clok!* Shoe off. *Clok!* Shoe on. I am aware of her thin little body wanting to be surrounded and protected by mine.

As I look around the room, the congregation seems motionless and far away. This stone and redwood church is modeled on a Zen temple, with cement block walls, high narrow windows, a huge redwood cross hanging high over the altar suspended from the stained glass ceiling. Once, during a sung litany, I thought I heard seraphim in a rainstorm just above and outside the panes of stained glass, the tips of wings sizzling when they accidentally touched. I saw the bishop look up at the ceiling the same moment I did.

Except for the preacher's voice the church is utterly quiet. The wind threatens outside.

Grace's shoes distract me again. *Clok!* Shoe on. *Clok, clok,* shoe off. Something is important in the *clok* sounds. Or between the sounds. Grace, my Zen master. Jesus could have turned at the Kidron Valley, away from the gate into Jerusalem. My prayer takes me to the threshold of this gate. If only I did not love more deeply than I can bear. If only my heart did not have to break to go through that gate.

"As a result of the Reformation...."

Clok! Clok!

An inner voice in my mind, not the voice of the preacher, speaks. "Let us also go, that we may die with him." I know that voice. *Thomas.* We are doing this because we want to be with him.

Against my lap Grace wraps the red chasuble around her like a blanket and falls asleep.

twenty-eight

Setting the Table

A friend gives me a bouquet of Lenten lilies and I arrange them with purple iris and ivy, and place them in the center of the bare oak table. I set the table for supper with white plates, burgundy napkins, small wine glasses, and a bottle of kosher Concord grape wine.

My family won't be going to the Maundy Thursday service at the church tonight, so I try to do something special at home. With the table set, supper ready, my Bible and prayer book next to my plate, I look over tonight's scripture readings once more before calling the family to eat. Pat and I have agreed to spend a little time at supper telling Bible stories. I like to tell them in my own words, with animation and voices, as if the story rises alive from the Holy Book, occasionally referring to the text for poetic phrases or quotes. I practice before I tell a story.

Tonight I've prepared the texts usually appointed for this celebration, starting with the institution of the Passover meal from the twelfth chapter of Exodus, when the angel of death is about to pass over Egypt killing the firstborn. Israel will be spared this plague if the people carefully follow the instructions given through Moses. After killing and preparing a lamb to eat, the scriptures say,

> *They shall eat the lamb that same night; they shall eat it roasted over the fire with unleavened bread and bitter herbs....This is how you shall eat it: your loins girded, your sandals on your feet, and your staff in your hand; and you shall eat it hurriedly. It is the passover of the LORD. (Exodus 12:8, 11)*

I will try to convey to my family how ancient this ritual meal is, and why the people had to eat in haste: men, women, and children about to escape from the slavery that had bound them for hundreds of years. You held a staff as you would if you were traveling, your sandals on your feet, your bags packed, eating hurriedly so you'd be ready if the signal should come at that moment. Some of you would eat with one foot already in the air, about to take the first step.

God commanded Israel to remember always this holy night and Jesus celebrated this meal more than a thousand years later and nearly two thousand years ago, on the night before his own passover from death to resurrected life. This meal becomes the celebration of our liberation from the slavery of sin and the fear of death. At that meal he took bread, blessed and broke it, gave it to his disciples and told them the bread is his body. Likewise, he passed wine to them, saying this is his blood. Jesus told his friends to remember him in this ritual meal because, as they would later understand, his body was broken and his blood poured out for them. Mysteriously, this wine and bread has nourished, inspired, and healed people, and even more mysteriously becomes the real body and blood and presence of Christ.

After celebrating the Passover with his friends,

> *Jesus got up from the table, took off his outer robe, and tied a towel around himself. Then he poured water into a basin and began to wash the disciples' feet and to wipe them with the towel....After he had washed their feet, had put on his robe, and had returned to the table, he said to them, "Do you know what I have done to you? You call me Teacher and Lord—and you are right, for that is what I am. So if I, your Lord and Teacher, have washed your feet, you also ought to wash one another's feet." (John 13:4-5, 12-14)*

Will my family notice how beautiful the table is? Having learned, as children do, through their senses, will they remember these tables set for Christian feasts? Will they remember the taste of lamb, the warm swallow of the wine, the touch of the oak, the mauve of lilies? Will they remember the stories?

I call my family to supper. They wash their hands (I hope) as I bring the dishes of food to the table and put Patrick in his high chair. Grace disrupts the saying of grace as she has every day this week: a laugh, a cry, a crash, a comment, whatever most disturbs at the moment and will guarantee a scolding and a trip to her room in disgrace. Patrick flirts with Jack and Jack responds by bopping up and down in and out of sight, slithering under the table as agile as a lizard. Obediently, he stops when he is told—until the next irresistible opportunity to make his brother laugh. Trevor sulks. He hates anything to do with religion. Always has. Pat sits sideways at the table, fidgeting, not fully with us. The phone will ring at any moment—an important colleague who daily disregards the importance of our dinner hour.

Grace watches from the upstairs railing and she is summoned back to the table.

The phone rings. Pat jumps from the table. Trevor now sits sideways like his father, ready to bolt. Patrick suddenly counts to ten and on the eleventh beat doubles over, his face pressed into his mashed potatoes.

Moses, the angel of death, and Jesus himself can't top that.

Trevor escapes, Grace has to go to the bathroom, the baby needs to be washed off. I still have Jack. As I take a washcloth to Patrick's face I ask, "Jack, what was this meal all about?"

"This is the night of the Passover in Egypt when the Israelites were saved from death and then escaped to the Red Sea and Jesus celebrated the Passover and gave the Lord's Supper the night before he died." I realize Jack listens better under the table than at the table. "Okay, you can go."

At my ordination the bishop asked, "Will you do your best to pattern your life and that of your family in accordance with the teachings of Christ, so that you may be a wholesome example to your people?"

I said, "I will," but I should have said, "I'll try." I'll set the table—what happens after that is up to them.

I bathe the two youngest children. They love their baths. We sing, tell stories, exchange jokes, get "baptized" under the water to wash the shampoo out of their hair. Then patting their skin dry with a towel, rubbing goosebumps, I put on their warm, clean pajamas and they're ready for bed.

I quickly change clothes and leave for church to do the whole thing over again: setting the table, sharing a ritual meal, trying to convey with passion an understanding of the meal to the politely listening congregation. A few will let me ceremoniously wash their feet. The congregation will be better behaved than my family, but the evening won't be as memorable.

twenty-nine
Good Friday

At the age of twenty-three my faith in God became a matter of life and death to me. I had looked into a horrifying emptiness during a clinical depression, experienced at the time as a loss of faith, and I never again wanted to suffer the anguish of life without a perception of God.

After my recovery I tried to pattern my inner life in such a way as to cultivate an awareness of the presence of God. Sister Allanah, a friend who ministered in the university's Newman Center, taught me the Jesus Prayer. With this discipline the words "Lord Jesus Christ, Son of God, have mercy on me, a sinner" became part of my walking, breathing, heartbeat. I learned to meditate, learned to listen to God in sheer silence. Like many new Christians, I was a little too pleased with my progress.

A nun called Sister Claire often listened to my enthusiasms and frustrations about prayer. She was a wise teacher, and we sometimes met at a table by the coffee pots in the seminary refectory, her bent, arthritic fingers clasped around her cup of tea. I told her that one experience of my life had troubled me so deeply I had never talked about it to anyone, and Claire offered to listen so that I could safely reveal the worst terror of my life up to that point.

The previous September I had entered the hospital in labor with my first child. When the fetal monitor registered possible fetal distress, it was decided that an emergency caesarian section would be performed.

In the rush of things, or by some stroke of fate, or through neglect, the anesthesia did not take effect. Naked, strapped down, tubes fastened to my throat and nose, a mask over my face and my arms outstretched, I attempted to

---

scream as the scalpel cut across my abdomen. I could not move or cry out throughout the surgery as I lay awake in horror and unutterable pain.

I could hear the doctors, nurses, and technicians talking and joking as they worked on my body, oblivious to my distress. I could hear a terrible, repetitious, grinding sound and feel a sensation of moving or being moved down through a backwards tunnel.

In the midst of the pain, the operating table, the casual operating room conversations, I had a terrible vision. In one moment I could see our whole planet from the time of primordial seas and one-celled organisms into the apocalypse and the end of time. I saw that everything about the universe was predetermined and nothing could change the course of destruction for which the whole earth was destined, including human life. I saw a world without God.

As time went on, this vision became more horrible to me than the agony of scalpel and retractors. I began to be aware of the coming annihilation of not only myself but the world. A backwards, steady progression of beats in time with the grinding sound I heard brought me closer and closer to the end. Annihilation would mean just that—no new life on the other side, no transformation, no redeeming of human history. No heaven, no hell, no space, no time. The world drawn into a single point and giving way to nothing.

If only there could be some kind of interruption, some break in this chain of meaninglessness, a skip of one beat, it could mean the existence of God. Then, I thought, I could bear the pain and take it to the end. I would even voluntarily bear the pain again, if not for myself then for the world, if only I knew it could stop for one moment, one pulse-beat.

But there was no God. No Christ. No break in the swiftly moving chain of death.

The last few beats of pain, noise, in mathematical precision, narrowed quickly. When the last point came I, and all the world, disappeared.

My husband said later he'd overheard someone from the operating room boast that the whole thing had taken only so many minutes and so many seconds.

I don't know how long I was unconscious, but I did not want to come back into the horror of the world, the horror of pain. I was hovering somewhere in darkness with a terrible fear of coming back into a world that I had been shown was an illusion, all the more terrifying for seeming to be real.

The nurse shook me. "You've had a beautiful nine-pound boy!"

Her voice drew me back into my painful body, and I replied with utter sincerity, with a truth hardly paralleled in my life up to then, "But that doesn't matter anymore, does it?"

After I had finished telling her my story, Sister Claire remained silent for a long time. Then she asked, "What was it that Jesus said on the cross?"

I wasn't sure what she meant.

"Jesus. Nailed to the cross, unable to move, naked, lingering in agony for hours. What did he say?"

"He said, 'My God, my God, why have you forsaken me?'"

Sister Claire looked at me carefully and said, "Even Jesus experienced the abandonment of God."

PRAYERS IN
SACRED TIME

Easter   ♦   Season of Union

Thirty
The Empty Alley

In the early years after my conversion, while I was struggling to understand the doctrines of the incarnation and resurrection, I hoped Jesus would appear to me on Easter morning to make everything clear. I waited—in our Washington, D.C. apartment across from the teaching hospital where my husband was a medical student, in our rowhouse near the slopes of Arlington Cemetery, where we brought Trevor home as a baby, in the small Texas tract house near the cow pasture where we lived during the time I was pregnant with Jack, in the Elmview Place brick house in San Antonio. Wherever we lived, I'd go out before dawn on Easter morning to wait for the Risen Lord.

I live for you. Show me yourself. Let me know for sure.

No answer. Just cracks on the city pavements near Washington Circle, jonquils by the gravestones in Arlington Cemetery, a curious cow in the pasture at the end of the tract houses. And behind the brick house at Elmview Place, the empty alley.

Finally, one Easter morning in Texas, slipping quietly down the stairs in the red brick house, I curled up in the wing chair, tucking my feet under my nightgown. I pulled the gray shawl I like to pray in around my shoulders, and I waited.

Early on the first day of the week, while it was still dark, Mary Magdalene came to the tomb and saw that the stone had been removed from the tomb. So she ran and went to Simon Peter and the other disciple, the one whom Jesus loved, and said to them, "They have taken the Lord out of the tomb, and we do not know where they have laid him." (John 20:1-2)

This moment in scripture draws me into it to wait, grieving for the places where I have prayed, where I have known Christ before but now no longer find him. Key people change, move, die. I mourn the places and ways and people in which I have found Christ: the oak woods, my mother's eyesight, early loves, feelings of closeness to God in the eucharist, sanctuaries in churches where I worshiped and then had to leave when we moved again. There is no clinging to one person or place that will be Christ for us.

Lex credendi, lex orandi, the church teaches, "the law of believing is the law of praying." The only evidence of the resurrection I have, finally, is the corresponding event that takes place in my own soul. Easter is part of a movement in my soul that began with my conversion, followed by years of Advent preparation and waiting. Eventually, the first elation of learning to perceive Christ through the light and clarity of Epiphany came to fruition, only to be followed by the inner labor of the dry, dark prayer of Lent. In those years, Christ worked in my soul so obscurely it was a secret even to me, the dry years masking a presence too intimate to perceive except over the long period of time it takes to get used to the darkness. Easter unfolds within this movement, within time, throughout years of purgation, illumination, contemplation.

Sitting in vigil is part of that. Prayer can be many things, but more than anything else prayer requires waiting.

By now I am so used to the darkness and waiting, waiting is enough, and darkness cleanses my soul to be receptive to what is Christ alone. In the darkness I feel something like trembling, a quickening of life in the depths of my being, like the first tremor of my unborn child, like a little fish nibbling on the line.

You have to go into the hidden places to watch. If Jesus had appeared to me in the empty alley, I would not have turned inward to look, to listen, and to find eternity. I would still be in the alley, still expecting something outside my-self—something that would go away before long, or that I might write off as a hallucination after all. Instead, I sit in the wing chair early one morning in Texas, my shawl wrapped around me, as if something was supposed to happen. I wait while the gray outlines of the room take form and gradually white morning sunlight fills the lace curtains.

thirty-one
Redeeming the Time

When I was a child I believed I was a fairy who had traded her immortality for the ability to feel human emotions and pain, and so became a mortal child.

I once confronted my mother with this theory.

"That wasn't a very smart thing to do," she replied.

My mother was good at ambiguity. I once asked her how it was possible for Adam and Eve to be the first man and woman on earth. Their son Cain, after killing his only brother, went off to the land of Nod, married and built a city. Who did he marry? Who needed the city? How did this story fit in with what the Leakys were doing in Africa, which we had watched on a *National Geographic* special on television?

"Well," she said, "Maybe Adam and Eve were the first *civilized* people on earth."

That idea kept me occupied for a few years.

I realize now how easily my mother could have undermined my love of the church and the Bible at a delicate stage, crushing my own inner sense of striving to recover my spiritual origins. Sometimes, I thought, she must have real-ized I was a changeling, despite family peculiarities inher-ited from relatives I'd never seen. Part of me was fairy, a druid in long red braids and jeans in the oak woods, still re-membering how to listen to trees telling me things.

When I think about how difficult the concept of redemp-tion has been for me to understand as an adult, I marvel how simply the idea came to me as a small child. By the time I was seven or eight I had accepted the neighborhood rumor that childbirth was the very worst pain you could endure, and I was determined to experience it because otherwise I could never be a real human being. Now, years later, when I hear in church that Jesus died for our sins, I feel confused. How could his horrible death buy back or pay off the debt of human sinfulness? How could his torture atone for things he had nothing to do with? How could a man dying restore hu-manity to the favor of the kind of cruel God who could let this evil take place to begin with?

For many years, Holy Saturday was the only holy day I ob-served inwardly with any understanding. I lived between my incomprehension of the necessity of Good Friday and my yearning for the joy of Easter Day. The first was a ritual ob-servation of the cruel and arbitrary; the second, an outland-ish feast celebrated by the well-meaning and weak-minded. The Old Testament scripture portion for Holy Saturday ex-pressed my desire for God, if there was a God, to withdraw and leave me alone.

A mortal, born of woman, few of days and full of trouble, comes up like a flower and withers, flees like a shadow and does not last....Since their days are determined, and the number of their months is known to you, and you have ap-pointed the bounds that they cannot pass, look away from them, and desist, that they may enjoy, like laborers, their days. (Job 14:1-2, 5-6)

Yet when I was a little girl, I wanted to experience the full extent of human pain for some reason larger than myself. What made me consider such a thing?

With the birth of my first child, I fleetingly understood redemption. Awaking from unconsciousness after a caesarian section performed without anesthetic, I hated the life to which I had been restored. I knew from my experience in the darkness that the world was a horrible illusion even more cruel for appearing to be so real.

My husband leaned over me describing our child. "Big. Nine pounds! Blond hair. A big nose! Strong!" I told him I had been awake during the surgery, so the doctor and anesthesiologist were summoned.

"Which way did I cut?" asked the surgeon. When I told him, he walked away without a word. My husband, still full of joy, accompanied me as they wheeled my gurney toward the nursery. Through the window I saw a masked nurse holding up a screaming baby. Arms and legs flailing, he wore a little tee shirt and diaper, a large bandage on the side of his head where the doctor's scalpel had cut him, too.

Time would not bend or break when I was bringing him to birth. But time would bend when I saw him. At that moment I knew him. I recognized this being, this human person, intimately and well. Not just because he had lived within me for most of this past year, but because I seemed to know him from the dark before time.

Was this the experience of an ordinary rush of hormones to my brain to ensure the bonding of mother and offspring? Was it prescience? Was it because I would know him someday? Did I know him from another time, or do I know him outside of time? Shall I ignore the experience or attribute it to a chemical impulse of the brain, or should I trust it as an experience of Easter faith? Easter is the bending of time to recognize what is beyond time.

All I know is that I already knew him. I knew Trevor. I also knew, even before touching him, that what I had just been through had been worthwhile. This knowledge of my child is what I think of now when I think of redemption. Did the birth have to be as savage as it was? I don't know. Maybe something was redeemed in all that pain. Still in pain, I knew it was worthwhile.

As a little girl I wanted to be a human being because I sensed that fairies do not die the way humans do. Fairies might become extinct, but they do not mourn. They do not feel pain or experience empathy; they cannot bear another's pain the way a human parent does naturally. In other words, they cannot love.

Mortality is necessary for love. Time is necessary for mortality. We are crucified upon the cross of time. Our loving redeems time.

thirty-two
A Discipline of Doubt

One year Trevor decided to come with me to Easter Vigil. This surprised me because from the time he was little he looked with skepticism upon religion and had been unmoved by the splendors of liturgy. He has always thought about morality and goodness and compassion; he is a good boy but not religious.

"He wants to come because I asked him to assemble the port-a-hose," observed his father.

Of the two older children, Jack seems more interested in religion. From the time he could pull himself up, he waited in the pew quietly until his favorite part, when the priest raised the bread and broke it. He seemed to know that this was the sacred moment when he could look beyond the thin white bread into some other world. When he was older, Jack let me preach my sermons to him on Saturdays and told me whether they made sense or not.

Trevor, on the other hand, approached Holy Communion with a bored objectivity from before he could speak. Perhaps he pays too much attention, is too focused and too critical. I think that if God's hand should ever snatch this boy and toss him playfully up through seven heavens and down again, Trevor would land with the dignity of a cat who for sheer embarrassment pretends nothing has happened.

But I was glad for him to come to the Easter Vigil and experience all the elements that tradition has evoked as the threshold of heaven: the new fire burning in a huge kettle in the front of the church, the Exultet chanted by the light of the paschal candle carried toward the dark nave, lesson after lesson telling of God's saving acts in history, chanted psalms and splendid music, the dramatic lighting of the altar during the Gloria, the Easter gospel, the clouds of incense, the eucharistic feast.

When it was over he grabbed my sleeve. "Let's leave!"

"We can have food, dessert, and wine in the parish hall. We're breaking our Lenten fast."

"Don't go in there. Everybody will want to talk with you."

"Just let me get a little to eat and a sip of wine, okay?"

"Okay, but don't talk with anybody. I'm tired. I slept through the second act."

On the way home, Trevor turned the radio to the local rock station. From time to time I turned it down, and when I wasn't looking, Trevor quietly turned it up. Then he said, "What happened in the tomb was pretty weird, wasn't it! What actually happened? Did Jesus turn to atomic energy or something?"

"I don't know. I think that something happened, but nobody knows the physics or the chemistry of it. Do you know about the Shroud of Turin?"

"Turin's in Italy. What's a shroud?"

"A shroud is a long burial cloth that goes over and under the body. There are scientists looking at a shroud that was used about two thousand years ago that has an image of a crucified man imprinted on it. It's perfectly proportioned—the sides are a little wider where the cloth covered the side of the body—and it's a negative image, you know, the opposite of real life, like a photo, or as if the body went through the cloth. The scientific team working on it isn't saying it is or isn't Jesus, but the marks of blood correspond to the description in the Bible—blood around the crown of the head, blood at the hands and feet, and blood at the side."

"Why do you think anybody would hang on to something like that? Some souvenir!"

"Well, what if you went to the tomb after having buried Jesus there and then came back a few days later and all that's left is the cloth his body was wrapped in? And besides, people are going around saying they saw him. Don't you think that if you found something like that you might keep it?"

Trevor turned down the radio a little bit. "Madonna's stupid. Mom, tell me some of the other weird things that happened after Jesus died."

"The best story—at least my favorite story—is about Thomas."

"Doubting Thomas?"

"Yes, but I wish people wouldn't call him that. Once Jesus appeared to all the disciples in a room together. He didn't open the door, just materialized."

"Like teleportation? How did he do that?"

"That's the problem. Who knows how? Anyway, everyone was there except Thomas, so later when he found out about it, he wouldn't believe them. Or couldn't believe them. He knew those other people really well and he probably thought they were just gullible and excited. But Thomas loved Jesus so much that he wouldn't believe Jesus was alive unless it was really true. He had to know for sure."

"And he got to see Jesus, right?"

"Yes."

We pulled into the driveway. Trevor and I hugged each other and he went to bed, while I began to prepare our Easter breakfast table and hide the eggs and baskets.

Prayer is not worth much if we do not doubt. Like Thomas, my son does not want to believe something that isn't true; he doesn't want to know God as a phantasm or an imaginary friend, or because he is afraid, or because other people say it is true. I understand this because at times I secretly agonize over how much of my own faith I have contrived, made up.

It is good to remember that to know God by "unknowing" is a tradition honored in mystical practice going back to Thomas himself. For my children, I do all I can. I can set the table but I can't make them partake of the bread and wine, let alone persuade them it is the body and blood of Christ.

thirty-three

Prayers Underground

I went to Rome with my grandmother at the age of nineteen as a tourist, visiting museums and monuments, memorials and parks. At the time I didn't know what I believed, but I remember the feeling I had on the train when it slowed down in the city as we approached the station. "Peter and Paul were here," I whispered.

Years later I went to Rome with other Christians as a pilgrim. We visited churches and monasteries, basilicas and shrines. We had come to pray.

Hundreds of miles of tunnels twist like a maze beneath Rome. Some of these were city streets that later generations simply built over, and some were catacombs, networks of passageways with burial niches carved into the stone walls. The catacombs became secret places of worship for Christians in dangerous times because the Romans considered burial grounds sacred, and they would not go underground to defile the dead. They did not expect Christians would, either.

But Christians went underground to venerate the dead, to be close to the relics of those who had died for the faith. The places of martyrdom and burial evolved into sacred shrines where Christians prayed to their heroes and heroines and begged for their intercessions. They came secretly to honor those who had passed through the great tribulation to complete their journey into God.

"Paul and Peter, pray for Victor." "Paul, Peter, pray for Erote, intercede." Christians wrote these prayers like graffiti on catacomb walls near the place where Sebastian was martyred. Because of these writings, many think that the bones of Peter and Paul were hidden at this site during the persecution of Valerianus, who forbade worship at the sites of martyrdom.

The intimacy of these prayers startles me. Victor and Erote and the others left behind their intimate prayers for coming generations to see. They must have been sure of the power of Peter and Paul and the other martyrs to intercede directly, to help and to inspire—sure as they would be of friends they could see or hear or touch. I might call a friend on the telephone and ask her to pray for me, but I'd phone only the closest of my friends to ask for such a request. Praying is an intimate act, especially prayers offered in the "great cloud of witnesses" in the communion of saints past, present, and future.

I was taught as a child that it was not only superstitious and primitive but sinful to "pray to the saints," as sinful as praying in front of a statue, which my grandmother emphasized was very bad. "People must think God is pretty stupid," she used to say, not without venom. I was taught to pray "directly" to God, through Christ, in the Holy Spirit. My cousin Dotty, however, prays to saints with real results. Her intimacy is such that once she got so frustrated with a particular saint she threw something at his picture. When Dotty loses something important (not just any little thing) she prays to St. Anthony to help her find it. Once her granddaughter Sarah lost something important, and she asked Dotty to pray to St. Anthony. "You should learn to do this for yourself," said Dotty.

"Okay," said Sarah, folding her hands and squeezing shut her eyes. "Dear St. Anthony, I'm the granddaughter of the lady whose prayers you always answer...."

I pray to God, through Christ, in the Holy Spirit, but I am not unaware of the influences of saints in my life like Teresa, Francis, John of the Cross, and Julian of Norwich who, like parents, have shaped my prayer and my life in Christ. Because of my observance of the Christian calendar, saints of the church are as much a part of my daily life as the people I see in passing when I shop or bring the children to music lessons and babysitters. I keep meeting the biblical personalities I love in prayer, like fellow travelers turning up at the same hotels.

I remember what it was like when I climbed down into tunnels and caverns, touching the cool Roman bricks with my hands, my shoulders brushing against the stone as my prayer crossed time, uniting with fellow Christians on pilgrimage and with Christians long ago and Christians yet to come. I entered houses through door frames representing ordinary lives, just as I live now, yet these Christians lived a hidden, extraordinary life I know only through the communion of saints.

A pilgrim is not a tourist. A tourist comes to see a place; a pilgrim comes to a holy place expecting to be changed. A pilgrim recognizes a holy landscape as a place mirrored within the soul. I enter the caverns of my own soul in prayer, descending into dark passages with desperate graffiti scrawled upon the maze of walls, with niches full of sacred relics grasped from pieces of my life, and with my soul's many shrines to saints and teachers and martyrs who have spoken to me in my dreams.

"Were not our hearts burning within us while he was talking to us on the road, while he was opening the scriptures to us?" asked the two men who met the resurrected Christ on the road to Emmaus (Luke 24:32). The cool, humid air sixty feet below the city touches me as I reach out to touch the lives of early Christians fearing torture and seeking heaven. I wonder to myself, did not my heart burn all those times, those many times I said the ancient prayers of the church, already joined with all the others beyond death and time in the communion of saints?

Did not my heart burn also, even that first time I came to Rome, unprepared for faith, and the train slowed, and I whispered the names of Peter and Paul?

thirty-four

The Labyrinth

They will hunger no more, and thirst no more;
the sun will not strike them, nor any scorching heat;
*   for the Lamb at the center of the throne*
*   will be their shepherd,*
and he will guide them to springs of the water of life,
*   and God will wipe away every tear from their eyes.*
*   (Rev. 7:16-17)*

Silently I light a candle and sit in the wing chair to collect my thoughts. When I reach for my prayer book to say evening prayer, a piece of school notebook paper folded tightly flutters onto my lap, with the word *PRIVATE!!!* scribbled in pencil.

March 23, 10:57 a.m.

Dear Suzanne Guthrie,

I understand that you are a minister. I want to know if people come to you if they have problems because I am having problems and I need to talk to you and ask God to forgive me. My grandfather and my grandmother died. My dad has been going out and coming home drunk. And when he comes home he doesn't know what he's doing and he's giving my mom heart attacks. My problem is that everybody keeps blaming things on me. My mom is hitting me for it. I am starting to steal money from my dad and spending it. I can't stop it's becoming to be a habit please help me.

Sincerely,
Angelina

It came with a packet of thank-you notes from a fifth-grade class who asked me to come speak with them on "career day" at their school, and I put it with the notes and newspaper clippings I keep for intercessory prayer in the evening.

Angelina's family lived off the military base in a remote trailer in the sloughs, as far away as it could have been practical for her father to commute to work. When I met her one day after school, Angelina told me about her father's drunkenness, his breaking everything in the house during his rages, his beating and almost killing her mother, the children hiding under the table while glass crashed around them. Angelina was sorry about the stealing and didn't understand how she could do such a thing; she thought she might be going crazy. I promised her I would try to help. "Whatever you do," she said, "don't let my father find out I talked to you."

Angelina's mother, who came from the Philippines and had difficulty speaking English, made it clear that the women's shelter in town was out of the question. I tried to tell her about the system of safety, the pick up and drop off, the obscurity of the safe-house, all the services, and the wise women involved in the program. I gave her information, phone numbers, procedures for getting help during his rages.

"No. No way. I must stay with my husband."

Calling the police was also out of the question. What happens to her husband's military career? What happens to the children? What if he isn't promoted? They barely make it on his pay now. What if he finds her and kills her?

The social services insisted this was a military problem. For weeks I tried with no success to alert the appropriate people in the military community of the situation, then confided the problem to a school administrator I knew. He was anxious to help, and began the same series of phone calls and visits and complaints that I had previously made, with as much success. Finally he was told to call the commanding officer of Angelina's father. When he was asked the nature of the phone call and described the situation, he learned a few moments later that he was talking to Angelina's father. Some time after that, the family was transferred away.

At night when I pray during the office, I pray for Angelina. I see her trailer home in the tall grass. I see other women and children, cut off from family, friends, support, and normal social activities by abusive husbands. I see women of entirely different educational and ethnic backgrounds at shelter meetings and workshops. I see women at a safe home in silent shock, or giddy with relief. I remember a woman up from the South buying enough fish for the whole shelter household and cooking it for breakfast, as Jesus did on the beach after the resurrection.

I see my next door neighbor, who never spoke to me before or after, waiting behind the lace curtain in my house for the police to come to escort her back into her house to collect a few things before getting out of town. I see a beautiful officer's wife after a wives' coffee whispering to me about her husband dragging her from one room to another by the hair the night before. I hear her say, "But he's not always like that." I overhear a commander say, "Just bring her some flowers and it'll fix things up. The little ladies like that sort of thing." I remember a conversation between the shelter director and a woman whose husband had narrowly missed hitting her with a marble table. She sobbed, "My pastor says it's against the Bible to leave my husband." "Honey," said the director, "it's against the Bible to commit suicide, which is what you're doing as long as you stay with him. So take your pick."

I keep Angelina's note in my prayer book and pray for her from the comfort of the wing chair. When I am feeling strong I pray for Angelina's father, which leads me into a labyrinth of evil and suffering begging for redemption.

Praying for Angelina and her father, mother, brother, and sisters leads me to other prison cells of the innocent and guilty alike, linked one to another by darkness, terror, and pain. I pray for hostages and prisoners by name, their guards and those who have betrayed them. I pray for children who are so affected by war that their inner landscapes are ruins of bombs and rubble. My prayer book is sometimes crammed with newspaper clippings.

Easter prayer draws us into a labyrinth of darkness in order to feel compassion more deeply. The resurrection makes it possible to travel through the labyrinth, as Easter draws all prayers into one through the cross. Intercessory prayer is not about ecstasy and visions; instead, it sends us out into the world to feel more deeply its unrequited love.

Angelina and I are linked to one another through prayer, but I can't touch her or whisper to her or comfort her. I have to go into the world for her sake and mine to comfort, to speak, and to touch. Love for her is the teacher of my prayer, guiding me to places I would have never gone, had I not prayed for her.

thirty-five
Prayers in Sacred Time

Thick morning fog from the coast covers this California mountain at Bishop's Ranch. The chapel bell rings and shadows move through the fog toward the white church. Time to sit and then first words, ancient words whispered in sleepy, early morning voices. A chill in the room, hard wooden benches, warm words.

Sunshine penetrates the fog. In silence I walk past flowers and the vegetable garden through pools of light between cloud. The kittens jump out of the grass and want to play. Time again to wait, watching the vineyards in the valley below becoming visible through the fog. Another bell rings.

Good food—no meat or fat, homemade breads, porridge, fruit—set out for breakfast. We eat in silence, slowly, each bite savored, time to eat, time to taste.

A bell rings and the silence is broken as we gather for a morning class on Benedictine monasticism, the pattern and rhythm of life we are to live this week. Topics on spirituality and the practice of prayer are presented by scholars and teachers, monastics, housewives, and business people, all men and women who live dedicated lives to God. Together we try to help each other find ways to bring back to our lives some authenticity of Christian practice. During the week together we follow the monastic hours of prayer and daily mass. We study. We have chores to do. And still there's time left over!

I am grateful for the resting places that have been given to me in my life.

Do not let your hearts be troubled. Believe in God, believe also in me. In my Father's house there are many dwelling places. If it were not so, would I have told you that I go to prepare a place for you? And if I go and prepare a place for you, I will come again and will take you to myself, so that where I am, there you may be also. (John 14:1-3)

When I hear this Easter text from John's gospel, I think of shelters along a mountain trail prepared by the Christ who has gone ahead to prepare the next place. Rooms full of time. Places to stop and breathe.

The "abbot" for the week brought a library of monastic and spiritual books and between times we can sit under the arbor to read, or pray in the chapel, or simply sit on a bench looking over the vineyards below and watching hawks circling in the sky. Later in the morning we study music and chant with a small "schola" of singers for the daily offices and special music for the eucharist. I play my flute. This is the only time all year I play my flute. It's not even noon yet and I feel I have already lived a full day. How is this possible?

Like most people I know, I never have a sabbath day. Sunday I leave early for St. Martin's to conduct a service, teach, do another service, make pastoral calls in the afternoon, lead the junior high youth group in the late afternoon and the senior high youth group in the evening. And if I didn't serve the church on Sundays, wouldn't Sunday simply suffer the spill-over from the rest of the week? It races by in a mad dash: keeping up with dentist appointments, school council meetings, boy scouts, cub scouts, piano lessons, saxophone lessons, drum lessons, swimming, tutoring, housework, cooking, laundry, potty training, shopping for food, buying endless sets of sneakers and school supplies, jeans, shirts, toddler clothes, keeping the schedules of two parents and four children from conflicting. Wouldn't I spend Sundays tempted to do at least the shopping and cleaning?

Once another officer's wife, a mother of two, sat on my porch, her chin in her hand, and said, "You know doing all this is impossible, but it's expected of us. The scary part is, we not only pull it off somehow, but we all work so terribly hard conspiring with one another to make it look effortless."

I never really have a sabbath except during a retreat. From the time of Moses the Fourth Commandment has required that the people of God set a day apart for the things of God. A sabbath day anticipates heaven. Early Christians moved their sabbath from the seventh day to the first day of the week to remind each other to stop, to live one day in time in the light of the resurrection, one day of the week lived as if time, sin, and death had been conquered.

On the sabbath you do not argue, handle money, or deal with the minutiae of daily life; you prepare meals ahead of time. The day is devoted to the beauty of holiness, of living outside time. Here at Bishop's Ranch I have time to remember that I am at some deep place attuned to the rhythms of resurrection. The circling hawks I love to watch are really turkey vultures. They eat roadkill and other dead animals, picking clean the bones and removing all remnants of decay, taking its corruption inside themselves to give back to the earth, and then they soar again. A naturalist once said to me about turkey vultures, "Look at them! You can't tell me they're just looking for food—they're playing. They're soaring and circling that high for pleasure, just because they can."

Mid-afternoon at Bishop's Ranch, time to do our "work." Mine is to practice my flute, which I do in the chapel. First I place a stalk of grass on the altar, a single gift from my walk to give back to God, and then I work on scales and exercises, learning again to breathe properly. I work on a little Mozart, Telemann, Bach, and then a very little offering of what might or might not be my own, a creaky, out-of-practice improvisation. I offer this, my practice, to God, alone in the cool chapel.

Miraculously, there is still more time before Vespers. I take my gray prayer shawl and slip away, through the woods and into the fields to find the highest point I can. A steep climb up through the very dry grass and caked earth takes me as high as I can be, far away from the brick house, above the giant tree house and the live oaks, the valley and vineyards, as if part of a civilization far away. I stand on the mountain, my face set against the hot wind. I feel it rising with power up the mountain to where I stand. I unfurl the shawl over my outstretched arms, the tassels like feathered tips at the end of my wingspan. I become my prayer, my soul rising on a thermal wind of holy spirit, ascending over the valley, circling with the hawks.

thirty-six

Altar to an Unknown God

For as I went through the city and looked carefully at the objects of your worship, I found among them an altar with the inscription, "To an unknown god." What therefore you worship as unknown, this I proclaim to you. (Acts 17:23)

We rise up out of the subway on the island in the middle of Broadway at Lincoln Center. Taking their hands, I can feel Trevor's and Jack's controlled excitement as we cross the street. Someone has given us tickets to a jazz concert, my children's first, to hear Miles Davis.

I used to come here and other places in the city as a young girl to hear music. My friends on Long Island and I grew up studying music, learning both classical repertoire and improvisation, practicing diligently, competitively, religiously. One of our shrines was a small basement den dedicated to a parent's jazz collection, where we worshiped the great icons of jazz on old seventy-eights and lovingly catalogued LPs. Another parent constructed a platform in his backyard where we played music together on Sunday afternoons in the summer. Sometimes I dreamed of moving to Europe to play in nightclubs, but there were too many other interesting things to do.

I was a talented but not extraordinary musician, and when the time came for me to stop practicing four hours a day I was relieved not to be a slave to my flute anymore but to enjoy it when I could. Only once in my adult life did I regret this, just after I had my third baby in five years. Exhausted, my body an aching wreck that would not heal, I sat one night on the floor folding diapers and armpit-stained undershirts watching the Grammy Awards on television. My friends had been nominated for a Grammy and I searched the audience of men and women in tuxedos and evening dresses to catch a glimpse of them. I suppose I envied them as much for the ability to slip into a shiny dress unadorned with spit-up or baby poop as I did for their musical achievement.

Most of the time, however, I am confident of my art even when I cannot or will not practice it. If music expresses the form, beauty, and balance underlying creation, then prayer is also an art. If music expresses the turbulence and imbalance of a difficult time in history, with arbitrary suffering and atrocity alongside beauty and joy, my mumbled prayers are a kind of art. Nothing in my life has been wasted as material for teaching me to pray, and music still teaches me.

Trevor and Jack shiver with excitement as we watch people come into Avery Fisher Hall and greet each other, the very old dressed up in suits and ties and fancy hats and floral print dresses like faithful churchgoers. I wonder if these are fans of Miles Davis, the old icon of jazz for four decades, or whether they just like loud electronic fusion. I wonder if they like Miles's new band or whether they just go wherever Miles happens to go.

As a young girl listening to Miles Davis's horn, those sustained notes that were never wasted, never superfluous or strained, but connecting all the harmonies around him with profound simplicity set a standard for perfection that I knew in some way I had to emulate. But if Miles ever meant to convey something sacred in his music, he never let on as far as I know.

I have been warned that I'll be lucky if Miles shows up at all, for he has recently canceled concerts at the last minute or refused to go on even while audiences waited. I watch my children's faces as the lights dim and the music begins. They gasp to watch the musicians work, to hear loud and live what usually comes softly from a small radio in our kitchen.

But I watch for Miles himself. He wanders onstage eventually in a shiny gold and silver suit, like a comic book superhero. The old fans cheer wildly with love but he does not acknowledge them, spending most of the concert fiddling with the dials on the synthesizers, his back to the audience. The music, when we can grasp it, is not memorable. The sidemen sweat, working to give the audience something. I feel embarrassed for them. Miles does a few uninspired licks now and then.

But then, near the end of the set, Miles turns around and plays. He plays one beautiful, sustained note carried over above and within the cacophony of his band and the machines with lights and dials that so preoccupied him. This is the sound I know. This is the sound that drew out my soul as a young girl to seek perfection, to seek union with unknown gods. I realize that I have always wanted my prayer to be like this—a clear, pure, protracted note.

Miles goes back to fiddling with the dials on the machines. My boys look bored and want to know when the next band will play.

St. John describes a vision of a place where there are no shrines and no temples, no need of sun or moon because there is only Light, and all light and all worship is the Lord God, the Almighty. For one short moment, listening to Miles Davis, I know this is true.

HOMESICK

Ascension ♦ Season of Unknowing

thirty-seven
Homesick

When I began to study theology I used to sit alone in the seminary chapel and take a sentence or phrase, often from the New Testament class I'd had that morning, and slowly let it work upon me. My task was not to figure out what the text meant, but to give myself to the words. As I got used to the chapel and to praying at the same time every day, I often felt as though I was being taught, although I could not have told you then or now what I was taught.

One day I happened to look up at the ceiling. Above me clouds unfurled in sunlight as if billowing in the wind, but instead of blowing in one direction they kept parting, layers of cumulous clouds revealing ever more beautiful clouds. I looked down at my lap and my hands—no clouds. I looked up; bright clouds billowed. I turned around and look at the back of the room. No clouds. I looked at the ceiling, where beautiful moving clouds continued to part and reveal more clouds. I laughed.

The vision lasted a long time, but eventually the clouds faded and I could see the ceiling clearly again. I left the chapel and went on to class.

When I told this story to a little girl named Anastasia, she said that perhaps instead of my looking toward God in my vision, God was looking at me. Or perhaps I was taking prayer too seriously and needed a good laugh. Maybe the parting clouds showed the layer upon layer of reality that is revealed when we pray the scriptures.

Praying this way brings back a memory of sitting by a pond as a little girl and staring at the water, where I could see three worlds, one upon the other. In one world, silver and gold fish swam one way and then another between long stems of pond lilies and grasses and decaying leaves. The fish stirred up sediment like dust in a sunbeam in the soft light of the water. A second world existed upon the surface of the water: waterbugs moving deftly across the pond, tangled islands of lilypads, the water rippling quickly in a breeze or vibrating after a fish jumped, pieces of bark, a feather and green algae floating with various and changing destinations.

The third world was the reflection of sky and clouds, blue and gray, moving and changing over the fish and grasses, the image broken by the sudden breeze and restored to perfection again, a sky flecked with pieces of wood and the feather floating between clouds. Some moments I could see only the bottom of the pond, at other times I'd see only the reflection of the sky, and sometimes I focused upon the surface world. I concentrated deeply to try to see the images of all three worlds at once, and sometimes I could.

What if you were a waterbug and could not see the sky, but only the horizon of the water? Or what if you were a sunfish, watching out only for prey or predator? What if you were a hermit thrush flying over the pond, never diving into the cold, dense water full of silt and light? You would only know one part of reality.

> *As they were watching, he was lifted up, and a cloud took him out of their sight. While he was going and they were gazing up toward heaven, suddenly two men in white robes stood by them. They said, "Men of Galilee, why do you stand looking up toward heaven?" (Acts 1:9-11)*

"Because we loved him," they might have said. Because we want to be with him and can't see where he is, and every time we think we understand, everything changes and we are left in the dark. We lost him once to death and now we have lost him to the clouds. We are homesick for him.

I have a friend who ascended to the clouds where Jesus was. Coming home from work around midnight, her van was hit by a car running a red light. Her scalp was nearly torn from her head and her liver was "pulverized," the priest told me. The next morning Priscilla's five small children walked bravely into church holding red carnations for Mother's Day, a custom of ours for honoring living mothers; white carnations remembered the dead.

For weeks she hovered between life and death, undergoing one operation after another. One afternoon my telephone rang. Silence. Then a feeble voice. "Suzanne?" I knew it was Priscilla.

"I'm not supposed...hard to talk...had to tell someone...saw him! Saw Jesus. Suzanne, he is so beautiful! We talk about the beauty of holiness, but we have no idea...."

She struggled for breath. "He told me to go back. Not in words. I begged him and begged him. I wanted to stay with him....He looked at me with such love and let me know I had to go back...something I had to do. Suzanne, he is so beautiful."

Priscilla eventually went home and gradually got better. I don't know why she had chosen me to tell her story to, but afterward I felt she had given me a strange knowledge. Like the waterbugs on the surface of the pond, all we could see in Priscilla's accident was tragedy. But at some unseen height or depth, it did not matter whether Priscilla lived or died. At some layer of truth, even if she died everything would be all right.

There are many things I will never understand. Like a hermit thrush, a waterbug, a sunfish, I am confined to one place. I know I live in California with responsibilities for husband, children, and church, and I long to go to a home I have never seen. I don't mean the place that the Air Force will send us next, but where Christ has gone before me.

thirty-eight

Cathedral Heights

I am asking on their behalf; I am not asking on behalf of the world, but on behalf of those whom you gave me, because they are yours. (John 17:9)

The harsh scrape of a chair pushed against a linoleum floor. Silence. The tap of a spoon against an egg shell. Silence. The clack of a toaster popping. The scrape of a knife spreading butter on toast. A cough. The click of a tooth against the rim of a glass of juice. The splash of coffee pouring into a cup. The clatter of the cup placed into its saucer. Silence.

The roar of my anguish peaks and breaks over the convent refectory, crashing into the silence, spilling and swelling into the empty corners. My eyes sting. Silence. I sip my coffee.

Tubs of very hot soapy water. Each sister washes her dishes. My hands want to linger in the almost unbearably hot water. Eyes meet, smile. More silence, except for the squeak of shoes walking from refectory to pantry to kitchen and back.

A tug on my sleeve. "Mother will see you now."

I wait in the parlor. I don't know what I will say to her. I've come to ask a simple favor: to ask the sisters to pray for me and for my family. That is all I have to say. Then they will pray for us, maybe putting our names on the bulletin board outside the chapel.

Mother Mary Cristabel enters the parlor. I try to speak. She gives me a kind look and holds out her arms. I sob until I'm exhausted, her shoulder and breast soaked by my tears.

The sisters will pray for us every day, for as long as it takes. This knowledge will carry me through my darkest times.

I go outside into the sunshine and cross Broadway, past book vendors, flowers stands, and shops, along 113th Street toward the Cathedral Church of St. John the Divine. Inside it is cool, dark, with sounds of chanting, but it is only the voices of visitors echoing through the giant vaulted ceiling, a ceiling so high it is like dark sky.

A friend once said to me, "When the time comes that you cannot pray anymore, the church will carry your prayers for you." It is that time now. I can't seem to pray for myself; nothing in my life provides a scaffolding to pray from. My marriage and my world are collapsing; Pat and I may divorce. Since college my self has been so intertwined with one other person I can't imagine what life would be otherwise, or who I could possibly be. If the marriage ends, then what? What about the children? What will we do and how will we manage? A busy household shatters at its very foundations. What took so long to build quickly perishes, like the rolls of an earthquake shaking the furniture, the plants, knocking the books off the shelves, rattling the kitchen plates, cracking the walls and beams and roof.

The solidity and sheer expanse of this building is comforting, twelve stories high with uninterrupted pillars soaring up to the ceiling—or is it really a building? More like a dream of rooms upon rooms. When my friend said the church would carry my prayers he meant that people would pray my prayers for me and I would float easily, resting as I am carried by the current of people in communion with God. But I can't see or touch the people praying for us.

This church building is itself an immense prayer rising from St. John's revelation, his vision of the apocalypse at the end of time. An angel commands John to write his vision. Angels bear scrolls with the names of the seven churches.

One angel holds the seal of the living God, another carries a golden censer. Michael guards departed spirits, Raphael travels over the world, Gabriel recalls the Annunciation, and Uriel, the angel of light, holds the sun. Two angels hold the morning star, seven angels hold seven vials, an angel shows St. John the heavenly city. Who knows what other angels roam this space?

I visit a favorite place where you can see the luminous Queen of Heaven, clothed with the sun and a crown of stars, standing in blazing light. It is as if she is so beautiful she has to be hidden among giant columns. I ask her intercession. I see Archbishop Cranmer reaching his hand toward the fire and ask him for help. Pacing the cathedral over and over, I let the church make its own prayer for me. The memorial sculpture for "Brother John Coltrane" makes me remember with thanksgiving how jazz once shaped my life. In the religious life bay I ask intercessions from the monastics through history who have shaped my prayer.

In chapels and other bays I softly sing a litany of saints, beginning with the Armed Forces bay. St. Michael and St. George, pray for us. St. Martin, pray for us. St. John the Baptist, St. John the Evangelist, St. Mary Magdalene, St. Teresa, St. John of the Cross, St. Angela de Merici, St. Julian of Norwich, pray for us. St. Patrick, pray for us. In the medical bay I remember my friends who have died and who have AIDS. I stop to remember the magnitude of suffering represented by the holocaust memorials in the pilgrim bay, and try to put my own little apocalypse into perspective. I find myself again and again at the Peace Table to be near the flame taken by a monk from the ruins of Hiroshima, trying to find some spark in the midst of the fear and sadness in my own life to care for and keep.

Once we visited Notre Dame in Paris, where the cathedral was completely dark except for thousands of candles lit all over the church—miles, it seemed, of candles. The older three children wanted to light their own, so I held Patrick in my arms as Pat gave the children *francs* and they each disappeared into the darkness.

Trevor was the first to come back, putting his money into my hand. "I really don't believe in prayer," he said, "so it's wrong for me to buy a candle." Jack made some private, deep, and heart-felt devotion somewhere in the church, something secret. Grace later told me that she lit her candle and prayed for all the blind people in the world, especially Grandma. She said she wanted to be an ophthalmologist like her dad so she could help blind people to see.

Jack and Grace and Patrick all carried some light, some memory or sense of God from this place, just as Trevor carried the memory of his profound wish not to defile the God-that-might-not-be-there. Somewhere in their own hearts a new heaven and a new earth will be born when this time is over.

But we are not living the end of time. I live in time with a breaking heart, swollen bones, frightened children. I pray for all the holy angels to guide the children when their parents fail, then walk out of the cathedral and all its vast space, leaving something of myself behind, knowing the cathedral will hold and carry my prayer.

PILLAR OF FIRE

Pentecost ◆ Season of Discipleship

thirty-nine
Downtown Express

Arms aching with the weight of my bag, I hurry past the flower stand, past perfect lilies and freesias, down subway stairs to the Cathedral Parkway station on 110th street in the late afternoon. Once in the crowded subway car, a voice laced with irony, a comedian's voice imitating an airline hostess, speaks over the subway intercom. "I hope you are having a lovely day. Those of you who would like a little change of pace might think about transferring at 96th Street to catch the Downtown Express. For those of you who are getting off at the next stop, thank you for riding the New York Transit System. Have a pleasant day."

Something wonderful happens. Spontaneously, the eyes of dozens of New Yorkers meet and everyone bursts out laughing. Animated smiles cling to our faces until the train stops.

Changing at 96th Street, we scramble for seats on the Downtown Express. One seat remains empty near the end of the car. From time to time people will sit there until they notice the stench of excrement coming from beneath the seat; as each one gets up and moves on, the man sitting opposite gives a beautiful, deep, and resonant laugh.

The subway car tears through the darkness of the tunnel and blasts into the light of the stations for a rapid few seconds, only to tear into the darkness again; light and dark, light and dark, the clap-and-screech rhythm of the subway.

A group of Hispanic women all talking at once sit directly across from me, while a tall Hasidic Jew stands in the aisle. On my right sits an Indian woman in western dress. Her little boy, about five years old, plays between her knees. The man across from the empty seat laughs loudly to himself.

Speeding through this dark tunnel scares me. I look to the faces nearby. The women across the aisle talk and laugh; their throaty, maternal voices remind me of my friends in San Antonio. I remember how my friends kept trying to put weight on my skinny body by giving me dishes of my favorite foods and foil-wrapped packages of tortillas. I always knew who prepared them because the taste of tortillas is the signature of the particular hand that makes them. At that difficult and disappointing time in my life the food was manna, God feeding Elijah in the desert, Jesus feeding the multitudes. I knew my friends not only loved me but supported my struggle to continue studying theology against many odds. Tortillas sustained my life materially, since I never seemed to be able to eat enough, but this bread was love and heavenly food from my friends and beyond them.

These women on the subway do not know me, but I feel linked to them through the musical cadence of their voices. I also feel linked to the Hasidic Jew, someone called to read the Torah, to take the scroll out and dance with it. So many times I have approached the Christian altar to lift the gospel book and carry it down the aisle. My eyes stinging, I have often wanted to turn and then dance through the congregation with the book. Instead, I walk down the aisle very properly, reverently, but not reverently enough. Someday, I think, I'll just dance.

When I see a prayer shawl, when I see a nun's veil, when I hear a chapel bell ring for vespers, I think we will survive. Sometimes I imagine that the idea of the *Lamed-Vov* is true, that the world is held together by thirty-six hidden righteous people. Instead of gravity, devotion holds together the world for the rest of us who are rushing through our lives. Maybe this speeding subway car would explode into thousands of pieces if people in hidden places all over the world were not at prayer.

I also want to be a righteous one, but for now others must pray for me during this severe stretching of my heart. My heart drops down stairwells and catapults up the cathedral spires into a cloud of hidden angels above St. John the Divine. It hangs suspended over city streets, caverns of darkness, my words snatched from my throat as if by a strong wind. My soul speeds through light and dark of the subway, the light and dark of my soul.

> *Darkness is not dark to you;*
>> *the night is as bright as the day;*
> *darkness and light to you are both alike. (Psalm 139:11)*

A man comes into the car collecting money for the homeless. The little boy near me has been watching me for some time. When I turn around to look he smiles at me, I smile back, and he blows me a kiss. His mother smiles. Underground, in the middle of New York, speeding through the light and dark of the subway, I know the ecstacy of belonging. I am the women across the aisle and I am the Hasid. I am the homeless man working my way through the subway cars. I am the mother and I am the diminutive boy with large brown eyes blowing a kiss. I am the laughing man across the aisle from the empty seat. We have become a prayer, one prayer hurtling through the dark to 34th Street and Penn Station.

> *And how is it that we hear, each of us, in our own native language? Parthians, Medes, Elamites, and residents of Mesopotamia, Judea and Cappadocia, Pontus and Asia, Phrygia and Pamphylia, Egypt and the parts of Libya belonging to Cyrene, and visitors from Rome, both Jews and proselytes, Cretans and Arabs—in our own languages we hear them speaking about God's deeds of power. (Acts 2:8-11)*

forty

Pillar of Fire

By now I know the feel of the sky so well I can sense fire in the grasslands of the Sacramento Valley. I can smell a fire many miles away, even before I go outside. Often I see only a thin pink line of old smoke resting low in the sky. Many times a day I trace with my eyes the outline of hills and sloughs and houses around me, watching for fire along the horizon.

Today one is burning nearby. Black smoke billows quickly and high into the air on the other side of Fairfield near the Air Force base. I have to go to the base to do some errands and pick up documents having to do with our move to Germany, where Pat will work at an American military hospital. Our belongings lie all over the house, ready for the packers and the movers, and the house is turned inside out, with the contents of closets and drawers lying in piles everywhere. Toys are stuffed in bags and books packed in boxes, pots and pans and dishes cover the counters, suitcases have been carefully packed and thought through for this week at home, the weekend up north, the days on the East Coast, the weeks in a foreign hotel, the months without our household things.

I step over piles of books, records, clothes, and dishes, car keys in hand. It is a relief to go to the car and away from the house, toward the fire.

The LORD went in front of them in a pillar of cloud by day, to lead them along the way, and in a pillar of fire by night, to give them light, so that they might travel by day and by night. Neither the pillar of cloud by day nor the pillar of fire by night left its place in front of the people. (Exodus 13:21-22)

When the Israelites sojourned in the desert, were they afraid at night when they saw the pillar of fire suspended in the air over the tabernacle? Did they ever get used to fire blazing over them at night and cloud billowing over them by day? When the pillar of cloud and pillar of fire moved, indicating that they were to strike camp and follow, were they reluctant? Did they get used to their campsites and not want to move on? Were they afraid?

Driving with the car window open, I don't hear the fire engines and traffic is not disrupted. Yet as I approach the base, clouds of heavy smoke billow swiftly into the air as if the base itself or the hospital were on fire. As I approach the rise where the hospital is, I finally see the flames—a long line of fire along the flightline where the dry grass burns. Firefighters hose the fire from trucks parked on the runway. Contained, safe, routine, and yet the sky is full of smoke and ash, waves of heat distorting the view of firetrucks and men along the flightline.

If I look to the future, I see nothing. No sign. No voice. By faith, I believe all will be well. Memory gives me courage to go on.

I remember driving toward Texas from Washington, D.C. in our blue AMC Hornet, with ten-month-old Trevor in the back seat, when the Air Force sent us to San Antonio. Leaving family, friends, seminary, the nuns who taught me to pray, leaving the wide leaves in summer and frost and snow in winter, a new landscape began to unfold. As we crossed the bridge over the Sabine River, I began to weep. We might as well have crossed the Red Sea to enter the desert—hour after hour of gray, flat land, barbed wire fences, and straight highway continued to unfold. I cried all the way to San Antonio. I could not imagine making a new life, or even finding God, in what Texans referred to as "God's country."

Those four years in Texas turned out to be among the most fertile and deep of my whole life. I saw much, lived much, gained many friends. I experienced deep and real prayer, coming to know God in a new way. And when the time came to leave San Antonio I wept as if I could never know God or have friends or pray again.

We moved to California and spent months with realtors looking for a home in a pretty valley surrounded by rich farmland. The realtor smiled one day, gesturing toward the hills, and said, "Welcome to God's country."

"Excuse me," I said, "but I thought Texas was supposed to be God's country."

"Well, you're actually right about that one, lady. Texas really is God's country because only God would want to live there."

God found me in California after all, and I learned to perceive God through the images of the new landscape: the hawks circling in solitude, the pillar of cloud in the relentless rains of winter, the pillar of fire in the firestorms of summer, the renunculas in my garden and the dry grass on the hills. Many places and many people revealed God to me. Although I can't imagine finding God in another place, I know full well that I will.

Still, I always hate to move.

King David, settled in his fine house in Jerusalem, wanted to build a permanent temple for the Lord, a "house of cedar." But God preferred to move with the people, to go before them in the pillar of fire and in the pillar of cloud coming to rest over the tabernacle. According to the specifications of Moses in the book of Exodus, the tabernacle was to be light and easily moved, made of tent curtains and a veil, acacia wood frames, an incense burner, a lamp, an altar, and other light furnishings. The ark of the covenant, which held the tablets of the Law brought down from Mt. Sinai by Moses, was supported by poles to carry it easily. The tabernacle imitates the heavenly dwelling of God. A God that moves.

If God dwelt in a particular place I suppose we would never have to move. We could build a shelter against the holy place and stay there. There would be no point in going anywhere else. Perhaps the prophet realized that if a temple were to be built to the Lord, it would become so sacred that the people would not go to the "ends of the earth" to find and serve God.

And so, once again, we are ready to move. I am going with my family to what seems like the ends of the earth. What is my life beyond the fire? What is God behind the pillar of cloud?

I only know that every time I have ever moved, I have had to learn to pray all over again.

Cowley Publications is a ministry of the Society of St. John the Evangelist, a religious community for men in the Episcopal Church. Emerging from the Society's tradition of prayer, theological reflection, and diversity of mission, the press is centered in the rich heritage of the Anglican Communion.

Cowley Publications seeks to provide books, audio cassettes, and other resources for the ongoing theological exploration and spiritual development of the Episcopal Church and others in the body of Christ. To this end, it is dedicated to developing a new generation of theological writers, encouraging them to produce timely, creative, and stimulating publications of excellence, and making these publications available widely, reaching both clergy and lay persons.